How to Give Your Child a Lifelong Love of Reading

First published 2020 by
The British Library
96 Euston Road
London NW1 2DB

Cataloguing in Publication Data
A catalogue record for this publication is available from
The British Library

ISBN 978 0 7123 5385 4
E-ISBN 978 0 7123 6785 1

Cover by Neil Stevens
Typeset by Sandra Friesen
Printed and bound in the Czech Republic by Finidr

How to Give Your Child A Lifelong Love of Reading

Alex Johnson

BRITISH LIBRARY

To Mum and Dad, Wilma,
Thomas, Edward and Robert

Contents

The unread story is not a story; it is little
black marks on wood pulp. The reader, reading it,
makes it live: a live thing, a story.
— Ursula K. Le Guin, *Dancing on the Edge
of the World*

Why reading is good for children

Reading is about falling down a rabbit hole, stepping onto the yellow brick road and going on an exciting journey into the unknown. Whether it's a novel or a poem, a history book or a science guide, a travelogue or a comic, diaries or jokes, a biography or a picture book, reading makes our children better and happier people.

Why? Reading is fun. It's an escape from boredom, perhaps to an alternative world or to an alternative way of looking at this world. It also offers children independence: they choose what to read – or what is read to them – and how fast to read it. As a small child, I remember my mum reading a book to me at bedtime called *Buzzy Bear Goes Camping* by Dorothy Marino. I enjoyed it, but

1

wanted to 'improve' the story, so I made her add some extra lines in pencil. They were nothing very dramatic, but I still remember the power of being able to somehow become part of the adventure and mould it in the direction I wanted it to go.

Children become readers when they find a book that they enjoy. And then another one, maybe along the same lines, maybe entirely different. And then another one. And another one. Once books make children happy, they are hooked for life.

Nearly fifty years after getting stuck into *Buzzy Bear*, I still enjoy reading for pleasure every day. And for nearly two decades I have been a parent myself, encouraging my three children to develop a similar love of books from their earliest days, introducing them to the delights of wordless picture books, reading to them at bedtime, helping them through the first steps of reading for themselves, nudging them to keep going when they discovered the delights of the screen and now watching them discover a wonderful new world of book possibilities as they hit adulthood.

The chance to imagine themselves in somebody else's shoes gives children the chance to explore who they are and who they can be. Sometimes a book can be a much-needed refuge. If things are not going well in a child's life and they are unhappy, books can offer more optimistic worlds where things appear gloomy but end up fine. Reading books can encourage children to consider and talk about difficult issues, help them to deal with the problem and build their self-esteem. The reading recommendations at the back of this book provide a helpful guide to suitable books, organised by age and theme.

Reading opens children's eyes to the endless possibilities in the world. It can sometimes be hard as an adult to remember the amazing sensation of reading something that truly speaks to you as a child, at a time when most of the world is still very much a blank canvas that is gradually being filled in around you. That feeling that the writer, even one writing in a different century, is speaking directly and personally to you as an eight-year-old. That feeling of meeting and getting to know a character who feels like a friend or a mirror image of the person we want to become. That feeling of discovering how a hummingbird flies or a car works. As adults, we are familiar with mysterious islands and secret passwords and shipwrecks filled with treasure. For children reading about them for the first time, this magic is still to be unlocked.

But of course it's not always about getting away. 'I don't believe one reads to escape reality. A person reads to confirm a reality he knows is there, but which he has not experienced,' said Lawrence Durrell, novelist brother of the animal-loving Gerald. By reading widely, children are learning to make the most of multiple viewpoints, assess them and come to their own conclusions.

Books also help us to understand who we are. The stories children read help them to learn that it is OK to be curious, a good idea to ask questions, normal to cry as well as laugh (hopefully laugh more often) and sensible to take advantage of opportunities or take up challenges, even if they can appear a bit scary at first. If you are wearing a magic ring of invisibility, why not make the most of it by having a chat with a dragon? Books bring children not only the unknown, but unknown unknowns.

By reading, they learn how to empathise with other people of all ages and cultures. How does Alice deal with an unexpected visitor? How does Badger manage the unmanageable Toad? How is *The Boy at the Back of the Class* made to feel welcome? This social intelligence helps them build relationships and get to grips with the nuts and bolts of how the world works. In some ways, reading is a solitary activity, but as it also helps children to practise what the world can be like and see things from another perspective, it teaches them sociability. It helps them become wiser.

Reading is also good for our children's health. A survey by the National Literacy Trust of nearly 50,000 British children aged eight to thirteen revealed that those who regularly read are three times more likely to have high levels of mental wellbeing compared to those who spend little time with their head in a book. Meanwhile, research with adults by the University of Sussex indicates that reading can reduce stress by up to 68 per cent. And becoming a reader as a child also has benefits for your children when they grow up. Studies suggests that people who read regularly enjoy improved memory function, are less likely to develop Alzheimer's disease and are more likely to live longer.

Whatever the reason for picking up a book, reading enlarges our vocabulary (figures indicate that children's books expose them to 50 per cent more words than prime-time television), improves our thinking skills and increases our ability to concentrate. Reading non-fiction opens up our children's minds to the astonishing natural world, the beauty of mathematics and the history that is shaping their existence. When the right book lands in children's lives at the right time, it can change their path forever.

Simply growing up in a home where there are books has a positive effect on your children's chances of obtaining higher education (it doesn't have to be piles of books). But it's also important to remember that not all child readers come from a reading family and that encouragement to read is one of the most important things that a parent can do, whatever their own level of education.

We will look at e-reading later in the book, but in the meantime it's interesting to note that research shows that in terms of how well you remember what you read, the traditional book is better than reading on screens. I know that as a child, I loved my *Nutshell Library* by Maurice Sendak, a very small four-volume boxed set that included an alphabet book, a book of rhymes about each month called *Chicken Soup with Rice*, a counting book and a cautionary tale. I enjoyed reading the books themselves, but I also took pleasure in simply taking the books out and replacing them in their proper places. My pleasure in reading them was very closely connected to my pleasure in holding them. Now I'm a little older, I have enjoyed sharing them with my young children and letting them hold them too.

It really doesn't matter what children read, as long as they read. There are books for all of them, including yours.

When I was a child I had one small shelf of books in my bedroom. Nowadays I have long shelves and wide bookcases in almost every room and an attic stuffed with heavy boxes of books. I buy books everywhere, from charity shops to select antiquarian emporiums, and I'm still a member of my local library too. Good books provide enormous entertainment, insight and information. They stimulate the imagination and increase empathy and understanding.

Though some keen adult readers come to books later in life, most passionate bookworms are given books at a very young age, and are read to before they can decipher words themselves. I have vivid memories of my first books. I didn't come from a wealthy or cultured family. I missed out on true nursery classics like *Peter Rabbit*, *Babar* and *Orlando*. I had 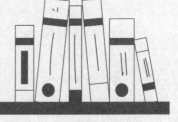 *Pookie the Little White Rabbit with Wings*, *Tuppenny and Squibbet*, a comic strip in the London *Evening Standard*, and *The Margaret Tarrant Nursery Rhyme Book*.

I loved this motley crew of characters, and when my parents were too busy or tired to read them aloud to me I looked at the pictures and made up my own stories. I flew with Pookie, I played with Tuppenny and her pet Squibbet (half a squirrel and half a rabbit), and I made up my own imaginary nursery rhyme world. The Margaret Tarrant illustrations were very dark and overly brown for a picture book, so my own adventures were sinister and gothic, but rather like Max in *Where the Wild Things Are* (my own daughter's nursery favourite) I was king of all these quirky nursery characters and quelled them with one look.

When I could read for myself at five or six I worked my way through all the Enid Blytons in the library, and read the Faraway Tree books again and again because I so badly wanted to be Silky the pixie. Then at seven I started reading the Mary Poppins books, *Katy* and *Little Women* and *The Secret Garden* and a handful of Nesbits. I particularly adored Noel Streatfeild's *Ballet Shoes* and for quite a while I pretended that I went to stage school with the three Fossil sisters.

I've carried on reading avidly throughout my life, at least two books a week. I wouldn't have written any of my 110 books if I hadn't been such a big reader. I feel like an evangelist for reading now. When children

tell me that one of my books made them start to love
reading it makes my whole career seem worthwhile.

*Dame Jacqueline Wilson is one of Britain's outstanding writers
for young readers. Over 40 million copies of her books have been
sold in the UK and they have been translated into thirty-four languages. Jacqueline was the Children's Laureate from 2005–2007
and is the Chancellor of Roehampton University.*

How to find good books

The first challenge in encouraging your child to read is simply to find books they are going to enjoy. A study by the publisher Scholastic suggests that nearly half of children find it hard to choose books they like, a figure which rises to nearly two-thirds among those who read less frequently (although their research also shows that nearly 90 per cent of children say their favourite books are ones they picked themselves).

USE YOURSELF AS A RESOURCE

The first person who can recommend something good is of course you. Even if it's a while since you read a children's book, there will still be some in your back catalogue which you feel are worth suggesting, and you may even still have them at home – my old collection of Asterix books has done sterling service. Before you dig out old copies of your own favourites, it's worth checking that they don't contain what are now recognised as negative racial or gender portrayals – *Tintin in the Congo*, for example, is certainly one to avoid, and later editions of his other adventures, such as *The Shooting Star*, have been updated. But essentially the task ahead of you is to build up your knowledge, and ideally some sort of home library, based on a wide range of authors and illustrators and from an equally wide range of sources.

One thing to beware of is imagining that just because you particularly enjoyed a book when you were young your children will enjoy it too. In her excellent memoir *Bookworm*, about her experience of reading as a child, Lucy Mangan talks about how her son Alexander often seems less engaged in what she was engrossed in at a similar age (to be fair to him, she did read *a lot*). This has certainly been my experience with all three of my boys. While my mild obsession with Tintin has been largely shared, my much-loved Jennings books by Anthony Buckeridge have had a much cooler reception, and the adventures of William Brown (another of my favourites – I still regularly reread 'The Bishop's Handkerchief' in *Still William*) have received an almost universal thumbs down. I still enjoy Alan Garner; my children have never done so.

ASK AROUND

Another way of approaching this is by word of mouth. Many of us learn about the best adult reads from like-minded friends and, crucially, people with differing experiences, who can give positive first-hand feedback about their current or all-time favourite books. As well as my wife, who tends to read a different selection of authors from my usual choices – so is valuable in recommending books which I'd probably not considered (or indeed heard of) – I have half a dozen friends whose opinions I respect and who also know roughly the kind of thing I like.

This can be similarly useful with children. In a general way, if their friends are reading something, this can create something of a buzz at school and encourage them to pick up a certain title. This push becomes stronger if it is an actual friend of theirs who is doing the reading or recommending, and can actually become quite competitive as they become desperate to read every one in a series or the latest release from a favourite author. And of course it's always useful to talk to other parents at the school gate about what the next book might be – books also make ideal birthday presents, and other parents will be grateful if you're quite specific about what your child wants to launch into as this will ease gift-buying issues.

From a publisher's point of view, Ed Ripley, UK sales and marketing director at Walker Books, is strongly aware of how key this is to a book's success:

> The elusive ingredient in a book's success has long fascinated publishers and to my mind it very much comes down to the clear premise of the book, whether it be non-fiction or fiction. The premise needs to be memorable, clear and ideally original in order for readers to chat about it to others long after finishing the book. From a sales perspective this makes the book's sales "curve" far less of a spike but maintains the book's sales at a higher level for longer. My experience of this most recently is with Angie Thomas's *The Hate U Give* – the book benefited from early US buzz, a strong marketing campaign and Angie herself visiting the UK. What has held the sales up at a high level has been, in my opinion, word of mouth: consumers talking about the simple, clear Black Lives Matter premise of the novel.

PRINT MEDIA

The traditional way to find out what's good, and especially what's new, is by reading reviews and features in newspapers and magazines. Sadly, impressive children's book sales – around one in every three physical books sold is now a children's book – and their £368 million market worth in the UK are not reflected in column inches in print. Nevertheless, it's still worth keeping an eye out, especially for the yearly round-ups each winter, and similar lists of suggestions for holiday reading in the summer.

The children's newspaper *First News* runs reviews of children's books which are written by the young people who have read them and also often includes book-related features and interviews with authors. There are various magazines for children, most of which include book reviews, but one certainly worth investigating is the bi-monthly *Scoop*, which has a different theme each issue and features plenty of original fiction and non-fiction. *The Week Junior* is a current affairs magazine for children that also includes book reviews.

GO ONLINE

Times have changed, of course, and while print is still a useful resource, there are many locations online where your children can find out more about their favourite authors and series. For example, if they enjoyed *The*

Wolves of Willoughby Chase by Joan Aiken, there is a huge amount of accessible material about the author and her other books at joanaiken.wordpress.com, while those who are keen on Ladybird books should definitely take a look at Helen Day's glorious site ladybirdflyawayhome. com (Helen is also active on Twitter and Instagram as @LBFlyawayhome). There are various general sites, but Goodreads (goodreads.com) in particular is worth exploring: while it is not specifically aimed at children, it does have useful sections on the latest releases, the most-read books and various lists, e.g. 'Best Books for Reluctant Readers', as well as mountains of readers' reviews. *Books for Keeps* is an online children's books magazine that has more than 12,000 reviews and 2,000 articles on its website. *Pen and Inc* is a magazine and listings guide that focuses on diversity and inclusion in children's books; it's run by CILIP (Chartered Institute of Library and Information Professionals).

BLOGGERS

Children's book bloggers tend to come and go depending on the ages of their children; they often start at the picture book stage and then, as their children grow older, the types of books they post about become more complex. This means that at a certain stage, the blogs simply end, although happily many remain online and are still useful even if they are no longer updated, such as the excellent playingbythebook.net. So, with that caveat, here are a dozen blogs written by parents, children's librarians and sometimes even children themselves to keep a regular eye on:

- tygertale.com
- readitdaddy.blogspot.com
- picturebooksblogger.wordpress.com
- librarymice.com
- minervareads.com
- mammafilz.com
- acornbooksblog.wordpress.com
- www.alongcamepoppy.com
- bookloverjo.wordpress.com
- librarygirlandbookboy.wordpress.com
- www.bookbairn.com
- mangobubblesbooks.com
- thebooksnifferweb.wordpress.com

PUBLISHERS

As well as independent bloggers, several publishers have useful sites which, unsurprisingly, focus on their own titles but are still of interest. These cover the whole age range of titles and include author interviews, giveaways, competitions, recommendations, news and quizzes. Among the best are picturebookparty.co.uk (Walker Books), epicreads.com (HarperCollins – also available on YouTube), penguinteen.com (Penguin) and readbrightly.com (Penguin Random House).

ASK THE EXPERTS

There are also several organisations dedicated to encouraging children to read. The Centre for Literacy in Primary Education (CLPE) is a children's literacy charity. Their work raises the achievement of children's reading and writing by helping primary schools to teach literacy creatively and effectively, putting quality children's books at the heart of all learning. Their free Corebooks website (clpe.org.uk/corebooks) lists a comprehensive selection of high-quality books for children from ages three to eleven. The lists of recommended texts are divided into age ranges and into three collections:

Learning to Read

The books in this section are particularly supportive of children learning to read.

Literature

For more experienced readers, texts in this collection offer an increasingly challenging range of material for individual reading or reading together.

Information

These are high-quality information texts that are interesting and enjoyable. They show how the text and pictures can work together to provide comprehensive information and an enjoyable reading experience.

The Book Trust (booktrust.org.uk) is the UK's largest children's reading charity and responsible for the Bookstart giveaway scheme. Its site has plenty of book reviews, 'if you liked this, then try this' suggestions, and lists such as the ultimate booklist to read before you're fourteen. The National Literacy Trust (literacytrust. org.uk) focuses on helping young people and families in poorer communities improve their literary skills, running a variety of programmes – often with schools – around the UK. Their online offering includes new research and resources for both parents and teachers. Last but not least, the Reading Agency (readingagency. org.uk) is behind the hugely popular Summer Reading Challenge and World Book Night, as well as projects such as the Reading Well programme, which offers reading suggestions that deal with mental health issues common to teenagers.

Podcasts

Dedicated children's book podcasts and radio shows are sprouting, offering a mix of interviews, reviews and stories read out loud, often including children talking about books they've enjoyed. You can listen to them via your favourite podcast platform.

Fun Kids Book Club is run by UK's children's radio station Fun Kids (funkidslive.com)

Down the Rabbit Hole (dtrhradio.com) was co-founded by Katherine Woodfine, author of the children's historical adventure series *The Sinclair's Mysteries*

Remember Reading from HarperCollins focuses on a single classic children's book per episode

Story Shed features a new story each episode written by primary school teacher Jake Harris

CBeebies Radio on the BBC website updates its podcast section daily with new stories

Just Imagine is a monthly podcast focusing on children's books, authors and illustrators at justimagine.co.uk/category/podcast/

MAKE USE OF YOUR BOOKSHOP

And of course as well as all these possibilities, you can also go straight to a library (which we'll come to in Chapter Six) or bookshop. Partly in response to the threat of online sales, but also because they love what they do, bookshop owners put on regular family-friendly author events, readings and storytime sessions, as well as building special areas in which children can relax and  browse or read. They will all be more than happy to recommend titles for any age group and interest.

Not only are there specialist children's bookshops, but many general bookshops also have well-curated children's sections. The following list includes those within the UK and Ireland, as well as international bookshops:

United Kingdom and Ireland

England

The Alligator's Mouth, Richmond, London

Bags of Books, Lewes, East Sussex

Blackwell's (children's section), Oxford

The Blue House Bookshop, York
The Book Nook, Hove, East Sussex
Bookwagon, Watford, Hertfordshire
Button & Bear, Shrewsbury, Shropshire
Chicken and Frog, Brentwood, Essex
Children's Bookshop, Lindley, Huddersfield
Children's Bookshop, Muswell Hill, London
Chiltern Bookshop, Chorleywood, Hertfordshire
Chiltern Bookshop, Gerrard's Cross, Buckinghamshire
Gosh! Comics, Soho, London
Heffers Bookshop, Cambridge
Kenilworth Books, Kenilworth, Warwickshire
Leaf Café, Hertford
Letterbox Library, Stratford, London
Multicultural Bookshop, Bradford
Mr B's Emporium of Reading Delights, Bath
Norfolk Children's Book Centre, Norwich, Norfolk
Octavia's Bookshop, Cirencester, Gloucestershire
Owl and Pyramid, Seaton, Devon
Pickled Pepper Books, Crouch End, London
Rogan's Books, Bedford, Bedfordshire
Round Table Books, Brixton, London
Simply Books, Bramhall, Cheshire
Storytellers Inc., St Annes on Sea, Lancashire
Tales on Moon Lane, Herne Hill, London and

Moon Lane Books, Lewisham, London
Tell Tales Books, Padgate, Warrington, Cheshire
Waterstones, Piccadilly, London

Ireland and Northern Ireland

Dubray Books, Dublin, Ireland
Hodges Figgis, Dublin, Ireland
O'Mahony's Bookshop, Limerick, Ireland
Tales for Tadpoles, Dublin, Ireland
Waterstones, Belfast, Northern Ireland

Scotland

Blackwell's Edinburgh, South Bridge
The Edinburgh Bookshop
Lighthouse bookshop, Edinburgh
Mainstreet Trading, St Boswells, Melrose
Topping & Company Booksellers of Edinburgh

Wales & Welsh border

Book-ish, Crickhowell, Powys
Booka Bookshop, Oswestry, Shropshire
The Children's Bookshop (second-hand), Hay-On-Wye,
    Herefordshire

Asia

Asia Books, Thailand

Eslite Bookstore, Taiwan

Kinokuniya, Singapore

National Bookstores, Philippines

Sketchbooks, Philippines

Swindon Books, Hong Kong

Australasia

Children's Bookshop, Wellington, New Zealand

The Dorothy Butler Bookshop, Ponsonby, Auckland,
   New Zealand

Little Unity, Auckland, New Zealand

Paper Plus, Dunedin, New Zealand

Readings Kids Bookshop, Carlton, Australia

Scorpio Bookshop, Christchurch, New Zealand

Squishy Minnie Bookstore, Kyneton, Australia

Where the Wild Things Are, Brisbane, Australia

Europe

Austria

Shakespeare & Co, Vienna

Cyprus

Soloneion Book Centre, Strovolos

K. P. Kyriakou Bookshop, Limassol

Meres Multispace, Nicosia

Denmark
Books & Company, Hellerup

Finland
Nide Bookstore Ltd, Helsinki

France
Shakespeare & Co, Paris
WH Smith, Paris

Germany
English Bookshop, Dussmann
Waterstones, Brussels

Greece
Benaki Museum, Athens
Booktique, Athens
Evripidis, Chalandri
Lexikopoleio, Athens
Politeia, Athens

Italy
Libreria Giannino Stoppani, Bologna
Libreria Todo Modo, Florence

Almost Corner Bookshop, Rome

Netherlands

Boekhandel van Rossum, Amsterdam

Waterstones, Amsterdam

Norway

Tronsmo Bokhandel, Oslo

Portugal

Baobá Livraria, Lisbon

Livraria Lello, Porto

Sweden

NK Bokhandel, Stockholm

Uppsala English Bookshop, Uppsala

As I work in a small independent bookshop in a thriving high street, I get to know everyone really well. I particularly love being asked to recommend books for children who aren't really into reading, for whatever reason. I prefer to chat with them, but often their parents come in on their own, worried and looking for advice. Reassuring them with all the latest research and my own experiences of working with readers is key.

Then I always invite them to bring their child in, since my priority is to ensure children feel good around books and reading. I try to make sure the children who visit feel no pressure, and can choose what they want, try before they buy and get something they are genuinely interested in. I try to make the experience all about them and what they want because reluctant readers often have experiences where they feel pushed into reading something they don't enjoy, find hard or don't see the point in.

I always keep a particular anecdote in mind when encouraging children to read. It is about a boy who thought books were not for him because he tried Harry Potter and didn't like it! This reminds me that it is important to offer as wide a range of reading possibilities as I can. It is one of the reasons I ask what the child is interested in generally, because if he or she loves sport, for example, then chances are we can hook them into reading through sport books. This could mean fiction or non-fiction, books, comics, graphic novels, audio books, magazines or even the sports pages of newspapers.

At this stage it is far more important to gift them new reading experiences, helping them to understand that all types of reading are good and that it's a pleasurable thing to do because you are reading about what interests you, not what you think you should read. Both of those experiences, once fostered and practised, usually lead to an association between reading and enjoyment, and a confidence in reading they didn't have before.

Cat Anderson is a children's specialist at The Edinburgh Bookshop (edinburghbookshop.com).

Starting to read

There are lots of tips and strategies in the following pages about reading to and with your children. If you use them every single time, you'll both be exhausted within a week and never want to see another book again, so pick and choose what seems right for you, and if something isn't working, remember that these are suggestions rather than rules set in stone. Remember:

- You don't have to talk about every book or analyse every character together – your child is not taking an exam on *Mr Tickle* or revising coursework about *The Borrowers*. Reading time should be natural and fun.

- When you ask questions, keep them open-ended. My sons really enjoyed a children's version of *Beowulf* but at no point did I ask them directly to discuss the changing notions of kingship in the poem (even though that's what we ended up doing, in a relaxed way, once we'd finished). Rather than 'Did you like that?' after reading *The Lorax*, maybe wonder aloud about how much a single person can achieve, which might lead to a discussion about Greta Thunberg and other young activists (see also Tracy Goodyear's comments on pp. 111–12 about asking open-ended questions).
- Reading does not have to happen at a certain time and place every day – bedtime has become a traditional time, but there's nothing stopping you from reading at breakfast, during the afternoon or around teatime.
- You can read food labels, car numberplates, street signs and advertisements anywhere, any time. Books are great, but *all* reading will help your child.

FIRST STEPS

It's never too soon to start reading together, even while your baby is still in the womb. Research indicates that reading to your child before they are born (especially during the third trimester) not only appears to relax them, but might also help with early language learning. Don't get too excited about giving birth to a baby genius, though, because it's more a matter of stimulation and help with brain development – playing music is also a good idea, but doesn't ensure they will be writing operas at playschool.

Once they do emerge, you can start with rhymes and simple stories. Obviously they will not understand what you are saying, but they will enjoy the sound of your voice and the images from books you are showing them. They will also learn how books function and will certainly want to grab them – especially if they make a noise or have a mirror – and probably nibble them too.

TALKING TOGETHER

At this stage, simply talking to your child in general is excellent for developing their listening and speaking expertise as well as their vocabulary. When I went shopping with my children in supermarkets, I used to keep up a running commentary about what we were going to buy, what the oranges looked like today, the price of beans and so on. But while talking is great, research suggests that reading to children is even more effective in improving their vocabulary and grammar – building blocks in advance of them learning to read for themselves. One study even suggests that picture books are up to three times more likely than conversation to include uncommon English words.

READING TOGETHER

Before you start, make sure there are no other distractions in the room, such as the radio, television or other screens. You want this to be dedicated reading time, not something to be rushed through or interrupted to deal with texts and emails, which can wait until you've finished.

However much you've been looking forward to reading *The Wind in the Willows* to them, that's a bit much for a six-month-old (I read bits of Samuel Pepys's diary to my eldest to try to soothe him to sleep – he has not turned into a Pepys fanatic in later life). It's better to start off with board books: wordless books made out of cloth or sturdy cardboard. Our earliest ones were essentially half a dozen pages of colourful or black-and-white patterns and shapes, with bits hanging off them to pull or rub to make a noise. All three of my children loved these, and they are certainly good for showing how books can be pleasurable items to enjoy from a very early age. While you're talking about what they can see, don't feel embarrassed to add in a soundtrack of animal noises or sound effects, which will make you both laugh – indeed, this is something you should carry on doing all through your reading times together to bring books alive.

DON'T GO TOO FAST

As your child gets a little older, instead of jumping straight in, it's better to chat about the book's title and what's on the cover. While you're reading, don't be afraid to stop the flow every now and again to comment on what's happening or draw attention to a picture – pictures can tell a story as vivid as the words on the page. Richard Scarry's books are especially good for looking at closely, with plenty of action in every square inch. Writer and illustrator Rob Biddulph's books are also a treat for little eyes to examine. As well as plenty of detail in the illustrations, they feature accessible rhyming texts and plenty of opportunities to join in and guess what happens next. His first book, *Blown Away*, is particularly lovely.

Indeed, research with three- to five-year-olds indicates that going slow can be very effective, and that pausing to give your child time to predict what word is coming next – and then pausing again after speaking the word, to let them consider it – improves the ability to remember and use the word again in a different scenario.

Even when you don't have a book to hand you can keep developing their sound and memory skills by singing songs and learning nursery rhymes together. At the early stages of reading, make sure that you are also selecting books that are playful and inspire children to enjoy fooling around with words and sounds. Those with repeating elements in the text, as well as actions, are particularly helpful in developing language skills.

HOW TO READ OUT LOUD

Don't forget to put plenty of emotion into it even when there are multiple characters each requiring a different voice. I enjoyed reading J. R. R. Tolkien's *The Hobbit* to my children but did find coming up with different accents and voices for all the characters quite challenging: the dwarves ranged from broad Yorkshire to my pitiably inauthentic attempts at Texan. Indeed, books with dozens of characters are probably not the best ones to start with; try something with a smaller cast list initially. Ones that went down well with my children with a smaller cast included *The Elephant and the Bad Baby* (words by Elfrida Vipont, illustrations by Raymond Briggs; three voices), *Tim Mouse* (words and illustrations by Judy Brook; four voices including a hedgehog), and *Mr Rabbit and the Lovely Present* (words by Charlotte Zolotow, gorgeously muted illustrations by Maurice Sendak; two voices).

If you're not familiar with the book you're planning to read and you've got enough time before you start, it's a good idea to have a quick look at it first and even practise reading some of it out loud. Professional audiobook narrators do not turn up at the studio on recording day without looking at their texts beforehand, and while you're not selling tapes of your reading sessions, it's still helpful to have some idea of chapter length and what characters are coming up. But if you make mistakes while reading, don't worry: it's supposed to be fun and you're not a machine. Your children will enjoy the story just as much, even if you mispronounce something or mix up the characters' voices.

As a general rule, in the same way that you usually need to talk more slowly when you're speaking in public to make yourself clearly understood, don't go too fast. Conversational speed is faster than audiobook speed so you should aim for the latter, especially when you start and are less familiar with the characters and the action. Sometimes you'll want to speed up to add excitement to the story, of course, or slow down where it's warranted, and you can also adjust how fast the characters you're acting out speak, a helpful variant when you've run out of accents. But in general, if it feels like you're reading too slowly, you're probably actually going at about the right pace.

Slowing down is also helpful since it allows children more time to understand unusual or old-fashioned words and complicated passages. As a trainee journalist, the first lesson I was taught when writing was to think like a reader. Similarly, when you're reading out loud, think like a listener – your son or daughter doesn't want this to be a broadcast performance; they'll enjoy it more if there's plenty of interaction and it feels like you're doing something with them rather than at them.

HOW OFTEN TO READ ALOUD

Try to read with your child every day so that it becomes, in a good way, a matter of routine. The numbers of parents reading to their young children every day has fallen significantly in recent years. A study by Nielsen Book Research indicates that more than two-thirds of preschool children in the UK were read to daily in 2013, but this dropped to just over half in 2018, with less than a third of children aged nought to thirteen being read to daily. Once your children start expecting and looking forward to a book at bedtime, you can see they are becoming hooked. Having said that, don't feel you have to read for a long time. If their attention starts to wane and they begin to seem bored, move on to another activity. Even if things are going really well, it's better to leave them wanting more than to stretch it out, so consider stopping at an exciting cliffhanger in the story.

Try to read for at least ten minutes a day (though don't beat yourself up if you miss a day or can only do less than that). If you can do more, that's great, but start at an achievable figure so that it becomes a regular habit and take it from there. Even ten minutes a day is more than an hour a week. If you make reading a regular part of your children's bedtime routine at a young age, you yourself may also find the later part of the day more manageable when it comes to turning out the lights. The Book Trust recognises this and has some excellent suggestions on its website as part of its Bath, Book and Bed campaign.

If you're reading a long book, don't be tempted to work out how many pages you're getting through a night, and how long it's therefore going to take you, in case it puts you both off. Some books you'll read in a single session (you might even read them twice or three times in one go), but others might take a week or even a month. And of course you don't have to read just one title: you can read a few shorter books at one sitting, or a short book and part of a longer book – any mix you like!

As your children get older, it's important to keep up reading during school holidays, especially in the long break at the end of academic years, to avoid what's described as 'summer learning loss' or 'summer slide', when reading skills can stagnate or drop off.

REREADING

It's good to get children to take part in the reading with you, so ask them what they think, or get them to join in with lines they remember or act out certain parts when you're rereading favourite titles. When I read *The Gruffalo* by Julia Donaldson to my boys, I always used to pause to let them finish a stanza: for example, I would read 'Where are you going to, little brown mouse? Come and have lunch in my ...' and they would finish '... underground house.' We read *Each Peach Pear Plum* by Allan Ahlberg so many times that in the end it became a feat of memory. I would turn the pages and they would speak the accompanying descriptions which they'd learned by heart. Sometimes I would deliberately get the order wrong so that they had the opportunity to scold me and show me how it ought to go.

My mother's pencil additions to *Buzzy Bear Goes Camping* ('Buzzy said, "There are some trees over there"') got incorporated into each retelling, rather than rubbed out at the end of the evening. There is considerable division over the question of how you treat your books, but the idea that they're a museum relic that mustn't be touched feels wrong to me. If your children want to add to a book, I don't see the harm. It means they've built a positive relationship with it. On the other hand, I'd keep any expensive Arthur Rackham first editions away from them if they're keen on the crayon.

One issue with constant rereading is that you may, entirely understandably, groan inwardly when they insist on reading *The Elephant and the Bad Baby* for the 300th time that month. I really liked Nick Sharratt's peep-through book *Shark in the Park* ('Timothy Pope, Timothy Pope, what can you see through your tele-scope?') and I would strongly recommend it, although if I'm completely honest, I don't want to read it again until the appearance of grandchildren.

But it's important to remember that your children are still finding intense pleasure in the retelling, so try hard not to show that you'd rather move on to something fresh. If it's obvious to them that you like books, it will make them keener to like them too. They like the security of something that doesn't change: try missing out bits and you'll quickly find that's not going to work. Your child will want the entire, exact story! We read a lot of Sarah Garland books together, and in *Going Shopping*, there's a scene in the supermarket where there are lots of fruits and vegetables on display. The first time we read this, we tried to identify each one. It was fun – some were more obvious than others, and some were entirely new to my boys. But after we'd read this a few times, I got a bit bored of doing the same thing and tried to skip past the pages fairly quickly. I was not allowed. We had to go over the same thing again and again.

Studies of language acquisition show that children whose parents read them the same book over and over again are better not only at picking up new words, but also understanding them, compared to children who moved on to new titles quickly. Research also indicates that when children reread books, how they talk about them becomes more sophisticated as they gain a better understanding of their complexities.

So grin and bear it, and although you'll be relieved when you can move on again, it's worth keeping some favourites around in case they fancy revisiting them.

IT DOESN'T HAVE TO BE YOU READING ALL THE TIME

If you want to try varying the reading experience, maybe an older sibling will be happy to read to a younger one, which is excellent for both of them in reading terms and also helps to strengthen their relationship, giving the older sibling a feeling of responsibility. Younger children often see their older brothers and sisters as role models; a role model that reads is ideal. Having an older sibling interested in reading often rubs off on the younger. The older sibling is also well placed to suggest other books to read in the future.

Similarly, grandparents can make ideal readers. The entire plot of the film *The Princess Bride* is predicated on Peter Falk reading a story to his sick grandson, who, though initially reluctant, enjoys it so much that by the end he asks to hear it again the following day. In the original novel by William Goldman, it's actually the father who reads the story to a sports-mad, non-reading, ten-year-old son, who is suddenly hooked for the first time in his life. The son explains how, though he could read himself, he loved the sound of his father's voice, and the book inspires him to become what his teacher describes as a 'novel-holic' as he races through countless tales of adventure such as *Treasure Island* and *The Three Musketeers*. Moreover, there are plenty of books in which the main characters are a grandparent and a child, which can make reading aloud extra special.

WHICH BOOKS TO CHOOSE

It's important that you try to offer books that are diverse so that children can see themselves and their peers mirrored in what they read, through characters who are similar to them or issues which are immediately relevant to their day-to-day lives.

The CLPE's Reflecting Realities report is the first UK study to look at representation in children's literature, and was first published in 2018. The aim of the study is to quantify and evaluate the extent and quality of ethnic representation and diversity in children's publishing in the UK. Of the 11,011 children's books published in the UK in 2018, only 7 per cent featured black, Asian and minority ethnic (BAME) characters, up from 4 per cent in 2017. Of these books only 4 per cent had a BAME main character, up from 1 per cent in 2017. Over a quarter of the books submitted only featured BAME presence in the form of background characters. BAME pupils make up 33.1 per cent of the school population in England. Research by *The Guardian* echoes this, suggesting that female and minority ethnic characters are appearing less frequently in illustrated children's books than male and white characters.

So while you're browsing, do consider race, gender, social status, disability, religion and geographic location. Look especially for work from authors who write about these issues from their own first-hand experience. *English Fairy Tales and Legends* by Rosalind Kerven features a dozen English fairy tales, each linked to a location or county, including 'The Dragon Castle' (Northumberland), 'The Girl Snatched By Fairies' (County Durham) and 'The Princess' and 'The Dark Moon' (Lincolnshire). For a feminist reworking of 'The Twelve Dancing Princesses' fairy tale, try Jessie Burton's *The Restless Girls*, and for a different perspective on Little Red Riding Hood, track down a copy of *Pretty Salma* by Niki Daly, which relocates the story to modern-day urban Ghana. This is equally important when it comes to selecting non-fiction. The nicely illustrated *Little People, Big Dreams* series created by Maria Isabel Sánchez Vegara celebrates women including architect Zaha Hadid, singer Ella Fitzgerald, civil rights activist Rosa Parks and entertainer Josephine Baker and is age-appropriate as well as inspiring.

Don't be afraid of taking a chance with some of the books you introduce to your children to give them an extensive reading experience, introducing them to genres and writers that they might not come across by themselves. This will mean some tricky choices. One survey found that a third of parents avoided books with frightening characters, citing examples such as the Grand High Witch in Roald Dahl's *The Witches*, and Cruella de Vil from Dodie Smith's *The Hundred and One Dalmatians*. Remember though that children can simply stop (or ask you to stop) reading if they find something uncomfortable. This is a safe environment in which they can find out what happens when things go wrong and try to work out ways to deal with these situations, sometimes by asking you questions about what's happening. I know several children who started racing through the Harry Potter series by J. K. Rowling, but then paused about halfway through when it starts to become a little darker, and returned to them when they were a little older.

Look on all books simply as books, rather than dividing them up into 'girls'' and 'boys'' books. Stories about action and adventure or ones that involve relationships and reflections about feelings should not be confined to a single gender. Girls do not all think alike, neither do boys, and stereotyping their interests is harmful in the long run, not to mention likely to lead to them reading fewer books. Young readers need a variety of books from which to choose. The Let Books Be Books campaign, a spin-off from the Let Toys Be Toys initiative, encourages publishers to avoid labelling titles specifically for boys or girls. You can find out more about it at lettoysbetoys.org. uk/letbooksbebooks/.

The CLPE suggests considering these criteria when selecting which books to read (clpe.org.uk/ corebooks/key-stage-1):

- texts that are multi-layered – capable of being read at different levels
- books that deal with important themes
- books in which language is used in lively, inventive ways
- books by skilful and experienced children's writers and illustrators
- traditional and contemporary 'classics' of children's literature
- stories with different cultural settings
- texts that promote discussion and reflection

LiTTLE BOOKS AND BiG BOOKS

As well as the type of book – fiction, non-fiction, poetry, comic – also consider books of different sizes. For smaller hands, smaller books are easier to hold, but they have some inherent cosiness about them too. We have a bookcase with weirdly variable and unadjustable heights which has a shelf on which a standard-sized Ladybird or Famous Five book cannot stand happily. Instead it's home to all the really small books that we've accumulated, including *Mister Magnolia* by Quentin Blake, *The Surprise Party* by Pat Hutchins, *The Father Christmas Joke Book* by Raymond Briggs, *Andy Pandy's in the Country* (one of mine from decades ago), *Katie Morag Delivers the Mail* by Mairi Hedderwick, a stack of Mr Mens and Little Misses, two copies of *Happy Christmas, Maisy* by Lucy Cousins, various Little Red Train books, various Noggin the Nog books (including my favourite, *The Omruds*, full of very small people), various Rev. W. Awdry railway series books, *A Child's Christmas in Wales* by Dylan Thomas with illustrations by Edward Ardizzone, *The Secret Path* (one of the Percy the Park Keeper books) by Nick Butterworth, and *A Rabbit in the Attic*, which allows the child to put their finger in a rabbit-shaped piece of cloth and poke it through holes on each page. These were all popular.

Similarly, there has been a trend in recent years for outsize books. One of the most popular hits has been *The*

Lost Words, a book of poems by the nature writer Robert Macfarlane and full-page illustrations by Jackie Morris which not only is an impressively large book to wrestle with, but also documents key words from nature that are starting to disappear. The huge *Maps* by Aleksandra and Daniel Mizieliński ('Travel the globe without leaving your living room') was also a big hit for a long time, partly because of the Richard Scarry effect, with endless details on every double-page spread to pick up on and discuss. *A Street through Time*, words by Anne Millard and illustrations by Steve Noon, was another success, following a Stone Age camp as it develops over the centuries into a big city. This one is a big landscape-format book, rather than a portrait-format one like *Maps* and *The Lost Words*.

READING ALOUD: AFTER THEY LEARN TO READ

As children start to learn to read for themselves, that's no reason to suddenly stop reading aloud. The CLPE strongly encourages continuing to read to/with your child even after they can read by themselves. Keep it going, every day if you can, but certainly as frequently as possible. It's still hard for them at this early stage, and you can help guide them over tricky bits or take over when they become tired with the effort of reading. At this stage, we had a lot of 'Can you read it now please?' If you keep reading out loud, it also means you can select books that contain intriguing stories or important themes but are still too difficult for them to read by themselves.

I remember very clearly my mother reading *The Midnight Folk* and *The Box of Delights* by John Masefield to me as a child, and if I close my eyes I can picture exactly where she sat in my bedroom and recall the 'one more chapter please' feeling when things got exciting. At that point I would have really struggled to read them myself, but they are still two of my favourite books. I didn't read them myself until I was in my thirties but I now reread *The Box of Delights* every Christmas. Young children's listening comprehension skills are better than their reading comprehension ones, so reading aloud is an ideal way of introducing them to new vocabulary in a relaxed way. They can sometimes grasp what's happening much more easily when they don't have to concentrate so much on simply decoding the words in front of them. As Sarah Mackenzie puts it in her book *The Read-Aloud Family*, a six-year-old just starting to learn to read won't be able to read *A Bear Called Paddington*, but they can enjoy it if somebody reads it to them.

Also, sometimes hearing a book being read out loud can emphasise elements that might be overlooked when children are reading to themselves. Certainly you should encourage them to think about what they're reading and perhaps ask them to predict what's going to happen. At the same time, talk about what's happening in terms of what it means to them, especially if there are subtleties in what the author is writing about. In her excellent TEDxYouth talk 'Why we should all be reading aloud to children' (available online), teacher and literacy consultant Rebecca Bellingham talks about how reading aloud can help the many children who find reading like a locked building for which they don't have the key, leaving them on the outside. She talks about how it can also work for children who can technically read well but find no enjoyment in what they are given. 'We want kids to get in the building and get to the party and stay there,' she says.

Alice Ozma is a good example of how reading aloud can continue positively well past the age many parents might think is time to stop. In her book *The Reading Promise: My Father and the Books We Shared*, she recounts how, when she was aged nine and living in New Jersey, her father promised to read a book to her every night for a hundred consecutive nights. They set off with *The Tin Woodman of Oz* by L. Frank Baum and one hundred nights later they got to *Be a Perfect Person in Just Three Days!* by Stephen Manes. They called it the Reading Streak.

But they didn't stop. They pushed on, first aiming at 1,000 and in the end stopping nine years later at 3,218 consecutive nights, finishing on the day Alice went to college. Along the way they took in Roald Dahl, Judy Blume and *Macbeth*. The experience gave Alice a love of books, but she also talks about how it helped her through the break-up of her parents' marriage and how the daily readings brought her closer to her father, especially as he often chose books which he hoped would help her deal with issues in real life, such as single parent families and bullying.

Do keep talking about books even once your children are reading by themselves. It helps them to understand what they're reading and explore the experience as well as developing their vocabulary – they will tell you when they want no more. Sarah Mackenzie found this while reading *The Wonderful Wizard of Oz* by L. Frank Baum to two of her children, who then started discussing whether a brain was more important than a heart, if they were forced to choose between them. Conversations can also develop about things outside the book: perhaps your own visit to the beach or something that you did at school when you were a child.

LISTEN TO THEM READ

Schools strongly encourage this, and it's a great idea. Many of the same rules apply in terms of letting them dictate the pace and the content: try not to interfere unless they are really stuck with something, and then start gradually, asking if they'd like a clue after they've had a decent time to ponder something or self-correct. Let them hold the book and turn the pages so that they have control over the reading time. And don't be judgemental when they make mistakes. Telling your child you're surprised they didn't know how to pronounce a word or what it means is not going to make them want to carry on: nobody likes to feel belittled.

When you've reached the end, make sure you tell them how well they've done and pick out something they did really well – maybe the way they voiced a certain character or puzzled out a difficult word or phrase. If you say something positive, they will want to read another time. It's important that you interact with the reading experience rather than simply passively sitting there and letting it wash over you. The more interested you appear to them, the more they will want to talk about the book with you.

Of course, these interactions can be fairly speculative. *The Sword in the Stone* by T. H. White is one book that especially lends itself to self-examination. In the story of the young King Arthur, Merlyn is aware of what awaits Wart (as he is known at this point) later in life, so he attempts to educate him about the ins and outs of kingship by turning him into a number of animals. In each incarnation, Wart learns a different lesson: about the relationship between brute strength and power (as a fish); the difference between age and respect (hawk); how absolute power destroys individualism (ant); democracy in action (goose); and the sometimes solitary life of a leader (badger). John Masefield does something very similar with Kay Harker in *The Box of Delights* when he is tutored by Herne the Hunter. You might ask your child which animal or attribute they think is the most important, or which animal they would rather be, and why.

ONCE THEY'RE READING FOR THEMSELVES

The key thing is that whatever they're reading, it should be a pleasure. Don't turn reading into an assessment or pick only books you think they ought to be reading or because someone else's child is reading them. Encouraging and suggesting books is great, but let them take an active lead in choice. In his book *The Pleasures of Reading in an Age of Distraction*, Alan Jacobs discusses how it's important to 'read at whim', to stop worrying if you're reading the 'right thing' and just read what you enjoy. He's writing about adults' reading habits, but the same thing applies to children. He's also scornful about the idea of 'Must-Read' book lists containing all the classics that must be notched up. You don't have to have read all the 'best books for a child under fourteen'. I liked Richmal Crompton's *Just William* and laughed like a drain when my mother read these stories to me. My children very politely can't see what all the fuss is about. Variety is the spice of life.

There also comes a point where reading serves other purposes apart from the literacy skills it develops. My boys ran through Robert Muchamore's CHERUB series with obsessional delight, and it was a good way of introducing them to more adult themes – the books revolve around a band of teenage orphans who are trained as spies and feature pertinent issues such as drugs, sex and violence, but not in a hysterical way. Muchamore has said that he has an '*EastEnders* test': essentially, he doesn't include anything that wouldn't also feature in an episode of the long-running soap. The books are not my cup of tea, but they're not aimed at me. My boys loved them.

AGE RANGES

It is important not to underestimate your child's abilities to get to grips with a book that you might imagine is 'too old' for them (and similarly, you might feel something is 'too young' for them, yet they will still enjoy reading it and get a lot out of the experience). The important thing is that you need to respect their choices, even if you think they're not the right ones – you do not want to put them off reading by appearing to be judgemental about what they've picked. If you are really unsure about their choice, then use it as an opportunity to discuss the issues involved. If they do appear to have bitten off more than they can chew in choosing something more demanding and look like they're losing interest, be ready to gently nudge them, by reading with them or even to them.

Books often come with age-appropriate recommendations, both in reviews and on the covers of the actual books themselves. While this can be helpful general guidance, don't feel restricted by this 'age banding'. It's much better to let your child choose something they feel comfortable reading rather than to ensure it is within official parameters. Certainly don't shame them if they pick something that is in a lower band. Conversely, just because a book is 'banded' for an older reader, your child may still love it (and of course, don't regard their reading ability as an opportunity for bragging rights; reading is not a competition to be fought at the school gates or via peeks into schoolbags during playdates).

SERIES BOOKS

Once they're getting the hang of it, series books often take root quickly in young readers' minds. I was hooked on *Alfred Hitchcock and The Three Investigators*, the Rev. W. Awdry's railway series books (partly for the illustrations) and Anthony Buckeridge's Jennings books, as well as the Tintin and Asterix books. More modern examples include Tom McLaughlin's funny *Accidental* series (*The*

Accidental Prime Minister was especially popular in our household), Piers Torday's imaginative *Wild* trilogy and Jason Reynolds' *Track* series – *Ghost*, *Patina*, *Sunny* and *Lu* – about young elite athletes. This quartet has particularly well-designed covers. You may well find that your child will reread series endlessly and then suddenly move on to a new series when Beast Quest or the Flower Fairies no longer enthral them. This is fine. Don't look on it as 'wasted' reading when they could be starting out on something new – they are still learning to understand what the story means, and if they want to go at it again, it means they are particularly engrossed in it. There's no reason to thwart that. Indeed, adults frequently reread books, and research by Costa in 2007 showed that not only do three-quarters of over-eighteens reread books, but that the top twenty rereads included childhood favourites J. R. R. Tolkien's *The Lord of the Rings* and *The Hobbit*, J. K. Rowling's Harry Potter series, C. S. Lewis' *The Lion, the Witch and the Wardrobe* and Anna Sewell's *Black Beauty*.

As well as series, also keep an eye out for sequels or prequels, or simply books by the same writer. In our house, there was a seamless move from Rick Riordan's Percy Jackson books to his other series, and from Cressida Cowell's *How to Train Your Dragon* titles to her *Wizards of Once* books, based purely on the enjoyment of their writing.

WHEN THE BOOK DOESN'T WORK

Try to keep things fun when you read together. A snack and a drink during a reading session works for adult book clubs, and it can also add to the experience with your child. If they're a bit fidgety, especially when younger, let them fiddle with their toys or their Play-Doh – they can be doing something else instead of sitting there rapt with attention and the words will still be going in.

Sometimes, though, it's obvious that it's not working out. Some books are simply more suited than others when it comes to reading out loud, particularly those that started life as tales told to the author's children, such as *The Tiger who Came to Tea* by Judith Kerr and Rudyard Kipling's *Just So Stories*. Kipling deliberately wrote this collection to be read aloud, initially to his daughter Effie. He explained how they came about in the *St Nicholas* magazine, when the first three were published in 1897:

> In the evening there were stories meant to put Effie to sleep, and you were not allowed to alter those by one single little word. They had to be told just so; or Effie would wake up and put back the missing sentence. So at last they came to be like charms, all three of them – the whale tale, the camel tale, and the rhinoceros tale. Of course little people are not alike, but I think if you catch some Effie rather tired and rather sleepy at the end of

the day, and if you begin in a low voice and tell the tales precisely as I have written them down, you will find that Effie will presently curl up and go to sleep.

Unfortunately, not all books you read aloud will enthral. Give everything a decent go but don't feel you have to carry on with something that nobody is enjoying any more. Some books may be great for your child to read to themselves, but not so great when read to them, so be open to ditching something even if it's had rave reviews from friends and critics.

LET THEM SEE YOU READ

At all ages, it's great if your children can see you reading too. If you spend all your time scrolling on your mobile phone, that's what they will learn to be normal behaviour. If they see you reading regularly, that's the lesson they will take away.

As important as reading strategies are in encouraging children to read, simply having access to books is very important – unsurprisingly, research shows that families who have more books in their home (somewhere between 80 and 350) tend to produce keener readers in the short term as well as improving their literacy in later life, with apparent positive knock-on effects for numeracy too.

The beauty of having a lot of books at home (and this is where your local library is also unbeatable – see Chapter Six) is that it gives your children choices.

They may like what you suggest, but if they don't, they can try out alternatives if these are easily to hand. This is why browsing in a bookshop is so much better than online – not only is it more fun, but your child can also get a feel for what might suit them without any input from an adult. You're encouraging them to read, but also to think for themselves about what they really want rather than what has been selected as 'good' for them.

Buying a lot of new books can be expensive (especially if your children demand the hardbacks as soon as they come out), so also consider getting them second-hand – I've been running the book stall at my boys' primary school for ten years and the pricing is pretty keen (also, I often let children just have the book for a token amount), certainly compared to the price of a cup of coffee. Second-hand bookshops are sadly starting to die out, but it's still worth hunting them out, especially on holiday, for bargains. Most charity shops also have a children's book section where the stock turns over frequently, so a regular visit often reveals new choices. And of course you can nearly always track down titles online that you're having trouble finding locally.

If children have plenty of their own books, having a bookshelf or bookcase of their own can add to their emotional attachment to them. I can still strongly remember sitting in front of my own first bookcase and just picking up the books and putting them back on the shelves, delighted with the idea of actually owning them.

And make sure you take books out: don't hide them all away. If there are books around the house, you and they are more likely to pick them up and take a look. Also think about how their books are being presented – if they're all jumbled up with their spines facing towards the wall then they are less likely to get picked, but if some of them are carefully placed face out so that their attractive covers can be seen, they are more likely to be chosen (an approach taken by many authors when they see their books on sale in bookshops …).

Being the Waterstones Children's Laureate is the kind of role that encourages you to consider your guiding principles as an author. My two starting points as Laureate were as follows. Point number one: books and reading are magic. Point number two: this magic must urgently be made available to absolutely everyone.

As an author, I want to write for all children; as Children's Laureate, I want to advocate for all children's right to access the magic.

When I began writing the *How to Train Your Dragon* series twenty years ago, there was a great deal of concern about boys' reading, and what we needed to do to get them more enthused.

Many parents tell me that my books have been instrumental in turning their boys into readers, and I have to say, although it is always a pleasure to be told your books have been effective, it has never been my intention to target boys specifically. I don't want to write either a 'boy's' book or a 'girl's' book, and I am wary of making generalisations about boy or girl behaviour because that can so very easily become a self-fulfilling prophecy. I haven't found the gender of the protagonists in my books to be an issue: I've lost count of the number of nine-year-old boys who say that Camicazi, the indomitable girl hero in *How to Train Your Dragon*, is their favourite character, and that is why I am so keen on boys and girls reading the same books: girls need to see girls like themselves being strong, dynamic heroes, and boys do, too. Therefore I do not have a 'boy reader' in mind when I write the books.

But I do have a 'reluctant reader' in mind. How do you get children – all children – to read for pleasure in an age when TV and film are beamed magically into children's heads without them having to do anything, but the whole decoding process of learning to read can mean that in a child's mind books come to be associated with something that is difficult or a 'struggle', particularly if they have dyslexia or another learning difficulty?

I work very hard to overturn that impression. I make the storylines of my books pacy, and thrilling, and I break up the text with as many wild and whirling illustrations as I can, to invite the child in, and to reward them for sticking with the story. I make the cover shiny and jewel-like, so that in the mind of the child the books are 'sweets', not 'Brussels sprouts'.

Transmitting the magic of reading to all children is a complicated and wonderful and frustrating and heart-breaking and fascinating and worthwhile task. It involves not only authors and illustrators but also a community of experts to get the right book into the hands of the right child at the right time. If your parents don't have the money to buy books, and don't go to the public library, and there isn't a library in your primary school, how on earth are you going to become a reader for the joy of it?

Research has shown that children who read for the joy of it have a huge advantage over those who do not. Every single child in this country should have the right to have a well-stocked school library, with a librarian who can help guide them in their reading journey. As Children's Laureate I am going to fight my hardest to advance every single point in the Reading Charter below, so that we can build a nation of readers, and the magic of reading can be made available to all.

Cressida Cowell's Waterstones Children's Laureate Reading Charter

Every child has the right to ...

1 Read for the joy of it
2 Access *new* books in schools, libraries and bookshops
3 Have advice from a trained librarian or bookseller

4 Own their *own* book

5 See themselves reflected in a book

6 Be read aloud to

7 Have some choice in what they read

8 Be creative for at least fifteen minutes a week

9 See an author event at least once

10 Have a planet to read on

Cressida Cowell is the current Waterstones Children's Laureate and bestselling author–illustrator of the How to Train Your Dragon *and* The Wizards of Once *series.*

I am a writer first and foremost because the wilderness I grew up in, in rural Scotland, made me one. Weekends spent scrambling over the moors, building dens in the woods and jumping into icy rivers fuelled in me an indestructible sense of wonder at the natural world. And it set my mind reeling with stories. Sometimes I wrote these stories down and sometimes I acted them out with my siblings but more often than not I just let them turn around in my head. I loved the fact that with imagining there didn't have to be a point to it.

At school, on the other hand, there were all sorts of exams and tests and end-of-year assessments. There seemed to be a point to everything. And for someone branded 'unteachable' and 'prone to spasmodic outbursts of tiresomeness' by their headteacher, this proved a challenge. I *was* a bit naughty (I see, in hindsight, that setting traps for your French teacher is unacceptable and stealing out of maths lessons to run wild in the forest is unwise), but at the heart of this wayward behaviour was another issue, one that didn't get 'detected' at school and that I only found out about years later.

I'm dyslexic. And whilst I can't pin all of my childhood misdemeanours on this fact, I do think it would have helped me to know that I think differently from most people – and that this is perfectly OK. More than OK, actually. Because it turns out that thinking differently is the key to thinking creatively, and to writing books. I never read aloud in class because the words used to jump around on the page, causing me to splutter out incomprehensible sounds. I used to spend hours decoding simple homework instructions because my processing skills were dire. And I frequently got myself into a terrible mess when trying to structure stories because organising information sent my brain into chaos.

What I was good at, though, were ideas – particularly in creative writing, and particularly if these ideas were rooted in things that I had seen or done. Cue my childhood adventures out in the wild. The places I explored back then existed in my mind in almost cinematic clarity. And perhaps they would have stayed there had I not discovered my local library and the treasure trove of books inside it. I began by reading fairy tales, everything from Hans Christian Andersen's 'The Snow Queen' and 'The Little Mermaid' to the *Fairy Tales* of the Brothers Grimm – because of Arthur Rackham's illustrations. They were

so exquisite I used to spend up to an hour before bed
every night simply looking at them. The illustrations
hooked me in but gradually I realised the power of the
stories themselves. I savoured the character names
(has there ever been a better-named villain than
Rumpelstiltskin?), I enjoyed the simplicity, familiarity
and repetition of the language, I devoured the
darkness of the plots and I believed, wholeheartedly,
in their magic. Eventually I craved
longer plots and so fairy tales
led me on to adventure books (a
map at the front was preferable
and the more badly behaved
the heroine, the better). And so I
discovered Jill Murphy's *The Worst
Witch* series, Chris Riddell and Paul
Stewart's *The Edge Chronicles* and
Philip Pullman's *Northern Lights*.
My childhood adventures instilled in me a sense of
wonder at our world, but the books I unearthed during
this time channelled this wonder into ideas with
shape and structure. They taught me an immeasurable
amount about life, too. Lucy Pevensie from *The Lion,
the Witch and the Wardrobe* taught me to keep on being
curious even when your elders have forgotten how;
Mildred Hubble from *The Worst Witch* taught me about

the importance of being kind; Roald Dahl's Matilda taught me that passion combined with determination can lead to all sorts of extraordinary things; and Lyra Belacqua in *Northern Lights* taught me that girls can be just as brave as boys, grown-ups and even armoured polar bears.

Illustrations were key to my falling in love with reading, but years on, visual prompts still remain vital to my writing process. I go on adventures in wild places to explore the settings for my books (writing *Sky Song* took me dog-sledding across the Arctic and living with the Kazakh eagle hunters in Mongolia, while every setting in my first series, *The Dreamsnatcher* trilogy, is rooted in the places I explored as a child); I lean on picture books, particularly classic fairy tales or stories illustrated by the mesmeric Jackie Morris, to build magical motifs; I flick through photography books to build magical worlds (like the sky kingdom of Rumblestar and the glow-in-the-dark rainforests of Jungledrop in my latest series, *The Unmapped Chronicles*); I visit museums to come up with fantastical objects; I play with Scrabble letters when trying to invent new words.

Becoming a published author didn't come easily to me. It took me seven years, three unpublished books and ninety-six rejection letters from literary agents

before I secured a deal. Then again, my journey to
becoming a reader wasn't straightforward either.
But thanks to a string of gloriously reckless heroines
I learned the power of curiosity, kindness, passion,
determination and courage – and those qualities
usually get you where you want to go, in the end.

*Abi Elphinstone is a bestselling children's author. Her books
include* Rumblestar, Sky Song, The Dreamsnatcher *trilogy
and, for younger readers,* The Snow Dragon. *When she's not
writing, Abi volunteers for Coram Beanstalk charity, speaks in
schools and travels the world looking for her next story.*

How to go places
The importance of non-fiction

When parents encourage their children to read, it's often fiction that first comes to mind and hand. Certainly most bookshops tend to base their children's sections on fiction. Research in the United States indicates that the average child spends less than four minutes a day reading non-fiction. But it's certainly worth encouraging your children to try it, especially if they're not finding fiction to their taste.

Of course the internet provides a vast amount of information but one argument runs that reading non-fiction books is more effective since it encourages children (and adults) to really consider complex themes at a steady pace rather than distractedly skimming and skipping about at speed. The traditional book method is more demanding but ultimately produces better results.

WHY NON-FICTION IS GOOD

In the same way that fiction improves a child's vocabulary, so does non-fiction

Even if it's a highly illustrated book, pictures can be useful aids in explaining new words and concepts in a few colourful pages. Or as Dr Seuss put it in *I Can Read with my Eyes Shut!*, 'The more that you learn, the more places you'll go'. They also introduce children to the concept of reading books and, especially importantly, teach them that books are enjoyable. For more on this, see Chapter Five, which discusses picture books.

It offers a different way of reading that may be more suitable to your child

Unlike a novel, many non-fiction books don't have to be read from cover to cover, or even in order – this means the child reading the book is fully in control, able to skip ahead, jump around and dictate the pace.

It helps to develop life skills

In a more basic way, learning about the world around them helps children with everything they may come across later in life, from applying for jobs to understanding manuals, and from decoding adverts to understanding timetables.

HOW YOUR CHILD LEARNS TO CONSIDER OTHER PEOPLE'S FEELINGS

Non-fiction also helps to teach children about approaching a subject with an open mind and learning about different points of view. Empathy is a skill that both fiction and non-fiction books can help to develop. Acquiring the ability to react emotionally to other people's situations, especially those facing very different challenges, is a vital skill for any young citizen in the twenty-first century.

The Diary of Anne Frank is not only a remarkable memoir of the realities of a life in hiding under Nazi occupation (dull food, and limited access to water and the toilet) but also includes complaints about her family with which many young readers will identify. For a good introduction to the current refugee crisis for younger readers, try *The Journey* by Francesca Sanna, a powerful story inspired by real life which has been endorsed by Amnesty International. More picture-led is James Mollison's book *Where Children Sleep*, which presents photographs of where children around the world sleep and, unsurprisingly, reveals terrible gulfs between their respective homes. Working with Save the Children, Mollison intended to encourage a response to how other children lived on the planet. He does something similar in his follow-up title, *Playground*, which looks at school playgrounds around the world. Note: the author has put many of the photos from these books, but not the text, on his website at jamesmollison.com.

An aptitude for reading non-fiction is especially important in an age of 'fake news', as reading skills help us to distinguish between what is true and what is dubious. Exposing children to analytical techniques and how to research a subject will help them grow up to be discerning adults and critical thinkers. Reading a variety of sources on historical events, for example, shows the importance of looking at multiple perspectives.

The UK's former Children's Laureate Malorie Blackman describes reading fiction as 'an exercise in walking in someone else's shoes for a while', which is equally true for this kind of non-fiction. This is why biographical non-fiction can be especially enthralling for children who love hearing real-life stories and may be less interested in the 'made-up' ones in fiction. Terry Deary's *Horrible Histories* are fact books with an inventive assortment of jokes, cartoons, quizzes, newspaper cuttings, letters, posters and plenty of gore and anti-teacher sentiment. This makes them very popular for children to read independently but difficult to read effectively out loud.

As well as the nuts-and-bolts 'how does a car work' type of non-fiction, there has been a boom in narrative non-fiction, which might appeal particularly to readers who already like a strong plot. These books use storytelling techniques – flashbacks, drama, first-person narration – to explain their material. *Hidden Figures* by Margot Lee Shetterly, which was made into a film in 2016, tells the story of the space programme in the United States through the eyes of four important African-American women. The book was originally written for adults, but there are now accessible picture-book versions for younger readers.

Non-fiction reading also encourages interaction. Reading out loud is certainly not confined to fiction. As you're reading together, it's easy to pause and discuss unusual facts or new theories as they arise and encourage your child to tell you what they think. Moreover, it can help make the link between reading and writing – your child might want to write their own little book about their favourite subject based on their own reading and knowledge, or set a quiz for you to take to see how you match up to their score.

Whatever you choose, the aim is to encourage your children to make connections between what they read and see and do to create a bigger and better world picture for them.

THE GOOD NEWS ABOUT PICKING A BOOK
You are pushing at an open door

Children are naturally inquisitive. They love facts and information, and they really do want lots of 'how' and 'why' explanations for how the world works. The right book can be genuinely inspiring to a child and raise awareness of issues they might not yet have come across.

There's a limitless amount of non-fiction, so there's something out there for your child

Fish, fashion, knights, video games, football, cookery, weird facts (children love anything weird or, frankly, a bit disgusting, so books that have an 'urggh but intriguing' factor are often very popular) ... the list really is endless and pretty much no subject off limits. Do you want something to help explain evolution to a son or daughter at primary school? Try Tracey Turner's marvellously titled *How to Make a Human Out of Soup* with illustrations by Sally Kindberg. Or the story of microbes? Have a look at *Tiny* by Nicola Davies, illustrated by Emily Sutton.

Non-fiction is a natural fit to the world around your child

My favourite book as a seven-year-old, one which I took out of the library dozens of times, was a history of the making of Stonehenge with lots of illustrations and slightly odd text fonts all over the place. I can almost feel it in my hands now, a slightly outsize paperback, partly held together by sticky tape due to excessive usage, and I can still see some of the pages forty years later. My youngest child at the same age was engrossed for weeks in a large book about maps and became fascinated by flags. By the time of the European Football Championships in 2016, he could identify not only all the participating

What can you do?

- Research your child's interests to find the appropriate title for them
- Use current events as a jumping-off point for picking an associated book
- Make time in your day to discuss your children's questions about their reading

countries' flags, but also dozens more from outside the continent. Many parents will be familiar with their young child's obsession with dinosaurs, so this could be a good opportunity to introduce them to archaeology or endangered species in the twenty-first century.

HOW TO DISCUSS THEIR NON-FICTION CHOICE

Whatever style of book you and your child have chosen, it's always good not to whizz through it as fast as possible, but rather to pause regularly to discuss the issues that it raises and connections to other books your child may have read. Ask questions that make them think about what they're reading or encourage them to look for answers in another book, rather than simply broadcasting information at them – think of yourself as a 'reading mentor'.

You might also want to consider taking a break and looking up something on the internet. For example, *Shackleton's Journey* by William Grill is a beautifully illustrated account of Ernest Shackleton's Antarctic expedition, partly inspired by the images recorded by the expedition photographer Frank Hurley. His hugely atmospheric work is easily available online and is a marvellous complement to Grill's superb retelling. And that search might in itself move to a discussion of the two World Wars, which Hurley also documented, as well as other related books. If you're reading *The Lost Words* together, have a look for videos of the flora and fauna covered in the book, or for the lovely album *Spell Songs* which it inspired. While you don't want to turn reading time into extended screen time, there's no harm in mixing the two a little.

MAKE THE CHOICE RELEVANT

One of the best ways of interesting children in non-fiction is making it a good fit for their lives. For example, if you're going on holiday, try to hunt down a couple of books that are relevant to your destination. If you're heading to Spain, *Katie and the Spanish Princess* by James Mayhew is a beautifully illustrated picture book which, while it is technically fiction, crosses over into non-fiction as it also works as a great introduction to famous Spanish paintings if you are planning to visit galleries during your trip. Major collections such as the Prado in Madrid have excellent websites with plenty of information and images you can look at alongside the book. René Goscinny's *Asterix in Spain* is a humorous romp from the north to the south of the country and older children and teenagers might like Laurie Lee's memoir of busking around Spain when he was just out of his teens, *As I Walked Out One Midsummer Morning*. You could also look on a map to track down your holiday home or destination, plan the route and look up interesting stops along the way. Maps, travel guides and travelogues can make the trip really come alive, connect the experience to the reading and increase understanding, making it more enjoyable.

If your child has enjoyed a film or a novel, they might be particularly receptive to a non-fiction book that adds further depth to the story. A *Star Wars* fan could be interested in finding out more about robotics and artificial intelligence; Michael Morpurgo's *Private Peaceful* leads naturally into reading about the history of the First World War; and the issue of Muggles and purebloods in the Harry Potter books could be a gateway into finding out more about racism. Sometimes it can be a small detail that sparks a new reading journey: in Madeleine L'Engle's classic time- and space-travelling novel *A Wrinkle In Time*, the thirteen-year-old main character, Meg, travels to a planet called Ixchel, which is the name of a Mayan goddess – perhaps a jumping-off point for looking at the Mayan civilisation. Additional background knowledge enriches the experience of reading and makes for a deeper understanding of any issues raised, both for you and your children. You certainly don't need to be an expert in any of these areas yourself to suggest topics in which your children might be interested – the world is full of parents with considerably less knowledge of castles and dinosaurs than their six-year-old offspring.

Non-fiction books also introduce children to different ways of navigating books. They can look for the main themes in the list of contents, drill down to details in an index and check on the meanings of key words in a glossary, not to mention decipher maps and get to grips with diagrams. Illustrations can be a particularly effective way of engaging your child's interest, so for younger readers, books that are picture-heavy rather than bulging with columns of grey text will initially be more attractive.

SCIENTISTS NEED TO READ TOO!

Reading is fundamental to academic success in a wide range of subjects, not just arts or humanities. Research by the National Literacy Trust indicates that the key factor in achieving good science grades at secondary school is well-developed literacy skills. Poor reading skills can have a negative effect on a child's attempts to understand scientific vocabulary and prepare reports of practical investigations. Indeed, our modern-day distinction between science and humanities subjects is not one that would have been recognised by the finest minds of the past.

DON'T FORGET GRAPHIC NON-FICTION

There are many non-fiction books that are heavily reliant on images, but a recent publishing trend has been the non-fiction graphic novel, which may appeal to children already reading graphic novels and enjoying comics (see Chapter Five for more on graphic novels). They also work well when read in conjunction with other books or as part of a wider education programme – a graphic history of Julius Caesar or Spartacus can bring ancient Roman history to life in a way that is not overwhelming. The drawings are excellent at helping children get to grips with the story and really make the action come alive. Good examples include:

Alastair Humphreys' Great Adventurers, illustrated by Kevin Ward, which features twenty fascinating journeys by a selection of diverse explorers through the ages from the Moroccan traveller Ibn Battuta in the fourteenth century through to the Apollo 11 astronaut Michael Collins and long-distance cyclist Dervla Murphy. There are plenty of maps, charts and cartoons.

Tunneling to Freedom by Nel Yomtov, illustrated by Alessandro Valdrighi, details the escape attempt from the Nazi prisoner-of-war camp Stalag Luft III, made famous by the film *The Great Escape*.

The 14th Dalai Lama by Tetsu Saiwai is a manga biography of the current Dalai Lama. This is one in a series of manga biographies published by Penguin which also includes books on Che Guevara and Gandhi.

Sally Heathcote, Suffragette by Mary and Bryan Talbot, illustrated by Kate Charlesworth, focuses on one maid's experience of women's fight for the vote, with a telling ending featuring her granddaughter.

Anne Frank's Diary by Ari Folman is an evocative graphic version of the classic historical text and features plenty of direct quotations from Anne's journal.

Suffragette: The Battle for Equality by David Roberts is a brilliant illustrated introduction to the women's suffrage movement and was shortlisted for the CILIP Kate Greenaway Medal 2019.

POETRY

Poetry is a standalone genre that arguably falls somewhere between fiction and non-fiction; but however you classify it, please don't neglect it. Children have a natural love of poems and recent sales figures show huge increases year on year, a boom which is in part down to sales to teenagers, with readers turning to poems to make sense of the world around them and to find voices that share their hopes and concerns. Poetry simply helps children to express their ideas in a short format that does not require a typical 'beginning, middle and end' structure.

Poetry, like any kind of reading, is for all young people and not an exclusive art form. Indeed, according to research by the National Literacy Trust, which runs the Young City Poets project, children who receive free school meals are significantly more likely than their more affluent peers to read and write their own poetry outside school.

Aside from reading and writing poems on the page, performance poets offer another way into appreciating the written word. Professionals such as Kate Tempest (katetempest.co.uk) and Caleb Femi (calebfemi.com), the first Young People's Laureate for London, offer a fresh and invigorating approach for young readers, whether they listen at a live show or online. Also worth looking out for are: Bristol-based Vanessa Kisuule (vanessakisuule. com), former Roundhouse and Nuyorican slams winner and the first Bristol City Poet 2018–20; Keisha Thompson from Manchester, Young Person's Producer at the city's Contact and an award-winning solo performer (keishathompson.com); and Leyla Josephine from Glasgow, former winner of the UK National Poetry Slam and runner-up in the Scottish Poetry Slam as well as a regular leader of poetry workshops (leylajosephine.co.uk). Their websites have fine examples of their performed work.

The Poetry Society runs the SLAMbassadors national youth slam competitions for those aged thirteen to eighteen (slam.poetrysociety.org.uk) and the Roundhouse performing arts venue in London runs several spoken word activities including an annual slam, the year-long Roundhouse Poetry Collective programme for sixteen- to twenty-five-year-olds, and the Last Word spoken word festival (roundhouse.org.uk). You can also find details of poetry slams at hammerandtongue. com. Apples and Snakes (applesandsnakes.org) is a major performance poetry organisation in England that also runs family events of interest. The Verbal Arts Centre in Derry/Londonderry in

Northern Ireland provides plenty of encouragement to young people interested in writing and performing poetry (theverbal.co). In Scotland, the Scottish Poetry Library (scottishpoetrylibrary.org.uk) runs a variety of youth projects based around poetry, including a fortnightly creative writing group for children under twelve.

'The sharing of poetry is such a great way in to children developing a love of books and reading,' says Deborah

Alma, who as the Emergency Poet runs the world's first mobile poetry service from the back of a 1970s ambulance. She has now set up in a bricks-and-mortar shop in Shropshire, and has worked extensively with schoolchildren as well as the general public. She says:

Quite often the best-loved early picture books are poetry; sometimes we don't even notice that it's poetry at all when we buy these early books. The really popular *We're Going on a Bear Hunt* [written by Michael Rosen, illustrations by Helen Oxenbury] with its repeated memorable refrains is a great example. Children can feel the regular rhythm and beat of the *We're going on a bear-hunt, we're going to catch a big one. We're not scared!* It has much in common with music or song. They can join in, they can anticipate what's coming next, they feel involved and smart, they feel it belongs to them, they can act it out, moving in time to the musicality of the words.

The best way to encourage your children to read poetry is by maintaining and developing the link from lullaby, to nursery rhymes, to picture books that are shared and acted out with a parent, to beginning to make songs and rhymes from the everyday stuff of their own lives. Encouraging the reading of poetry up and into primary school is relatively easy. Children love the music and range and playfulness of poetry.

Encouraging children beyond the sharing of poetry books with a parent or in school is more difficult. As adults few of us regularly read poetry and for me I think it's really important to get the right collection or anthology to the right child. Poetry is as diverse as fiction and we would not necessarily expect the lover of horse stories to read dystopian future fiction. So it is with poetry. This might need some curating on the part of a parent or teacher. Important here too is the teaching of poetry, and encouraging children to write their own is the best way for them to 'get it' and love it. There are some excellent poetry anthologies out there, but still too many that are stodgy and old-fashioned, with a very adult view of what children should be reading.

Deborah feels that there is a different challenge in terms of poetry at secondary school, where she says the reading of poetry has largely been to pull apart an often archaic poetic text for the demands of the curriculum. 'This can have a very off-putting effect,' she says. 'Small changes in the curriculum might allow for a more contemporary engagement with poets and performers online, for example, and including some creative element in assessments might help here. But young people are finding their own way to poetry through online places like Instagram and performance poets on YouTube.'

If you're not sure where to start when looking for poetry, there are plenty of people out there who are very happy to help, including:

The CLPE, which is the National Poetry Centre for Primary Schools. They have a long history of recommending poetry collections and anthologies and run the CLIPPA award, which is the only award for published children's poetry in the UK. The award also has a shadowing scheme designed to engage children in performing poetry.

Poetryline, run by the CLPE (clpe.org.uk/poetryline), contains a wealth of resources for schools but also has videos of a wide range of published poets performing poetry and talking about poetry that parents and children can access.

The Poetry Foundation (poetryfoundation.org) has plenty of information about poetry in general and sections for children.

The Children's Poetry Archive (childrens.poetryarchive. org) provides new and classic poems in readings, some by their authors (including performance poet Joseph Coelho), that have been specially recorded for the site.

The Poetry Book Society (poetrybooks.co.uk) has a useful children's poetry corner.

The Poetry Society (poetrysociety.org.uk) and the National Poetry Library (nationalpoetrylibrary.org.uk) run lots of events and poetry programmes, and the latter

What can you do?

Share poetry and the reading of poetry books together. When I was a teenager, my father used to wake me up in the morning by opening the curtains of my bedroom and declaiming from the start of *The Rubáiyát of Omar Khayyám*: 'Awake! for morning in the bowl of night has flung the stone that puts the stars to flight.' To be honest, I've never actually read it, but the result of those months of repetition is that I can still quote the first two lines quite impressively more than thirty years later.

Just have poetry around: print out a poem and stick it on the fridge, or memorise some together.

Find poems that speak to something in your child's life.

Don't expect children to sit and read a poetry book from cover to cover. One poem at a time is good, so leave poetry books in the bathroom, on the coffee table or in the kitchen, just to dip into.

actively encourages visits from families, providing help and information for parents with under-fives as well as for older children keen on writing poetry themselves.

Anthologies of poems are also a good place to start, as they allow your child the chance to pick and choose from a wide variety of styles and voices and start to find favourite poets to explore further. One of the most popular is *The Rattle Bag* co-edited by Seamus Heaney and Ted Hughes, though my children particularly liked *Read Me and Laugh: A Funny Poem for Every Day of the Year* edited by Gaby Morgan, and one from my own childhood, *Four Feet and Two* compiled by Leila Berg, full of poems about animals and nature (sadly this is out of print now, so needs to be sourced second-hand). And don't be put off by the seemingly narrow title of *England: Poems from a School* edited by Kate Clanchy. Kate is the writer in residence at the Oxford Spires Academy and works with its pupils, who have a huge variety of international backgrounds, to write and publish their own outstanding poems. Kate also tweets examples of their work at @KateClanchy1.

When I was twenty-six years old, I paid to get into my own poetry gig. I walked up to the door of the venue and the person on the door said, 'It's £5', and I panicked and was too embarrassed to say that I was actually the one performing that night, so I paid £5 and went in.

The reason I say this is because, even after actually working in poetry for about three years by then, I still felt intimidated by spaces where poetry was 'happening'. I still felt a bit like it was some sort of private club that I shouldn't really be in and where you needed to know all the codes to understand what was happening.

I don't know where this idea came from but it happened, for me, at the age of about eleven. Before that, I had always felt that poetry was just like any other type of writing. It was no more intimidating than bedtime stories. It *was* bedtime stories.

I don't remember my favourite poets as a kid but I do remember my favourite poems. 'Please Mrs Butler' (by Allan Ahlberg) was my number one, then 'When Betty Eats Spaghetti' and another called 'I Don't Want to Go into School Today Mum' by Colin McNaughton.

I remember the books these poems were in as much as the poems. They were fun too. *Please Mrs Butler* was a miniature book, in a miniature box with four other tiny books of poetry inside. I loved reading these because my teddies and Barbies could also read them. The other poems were in an anthology, full of colourful pictures.

Those were the only poetry books I had, but they were enough. I reread them a lot. I didn't like all the poems, but I liked enough of them. I liked poetry and I wasn't afraid to admit that.

As I got older, I suddenly stopped. From about the age of eleven to twenty, I found little poetry I could relate to. It became either too silly and childish or too obscure.

At school, we picked poetry apart in lessons like a medical procedure. I didn't realise we could enjoy poems any more. Unlike with films and TV programmes and novels and short stories, I also started to feel intimidated at the idea of having opinions about poetry. If I didn't like a poem, I assumed it was because I was too stupid to understand it.

Weirdly, whilst feeling excluded from poetry, I still always wrote. I wrote my diaries in poems all through my late childhood and teens (and still to this day), but I didn't equate what I was doing with a love of poetry. I printed off song lyrics which I loved and read them like novels, but I didn't equate this with a love of poetry either.

There wasn't a set moment when I started feeling less intimidated by poetry. I think it just eased with practice. I went to my first open mic and watched people reading poems to other people. The more readings I went to, the more I realised that poets were not people in berets (or could be, but didn't have to be) who only wore black polo necks and scoffed at anyone who didn't know the entire works of Maya Angelou or Ted Hughes. Similarly, 'performance' poets, who I like to just call poets as well, were not all stage-hungry show-offs who knew nothing of the written word. They were mainly just people who liked to read and write poems. And the variety of poems they wrote and read was as diverse as the music people like or the paintings we might admire.

I still have people email me, scared to come to a poetry reading I'm doing, because they're not really a 'poetry person' or don't know 'the etiquette'. Similarly, if people enjoyed a gig, they often caveat it with 'I don't know anything about poetry, but ...'. I don't know how to dance the quick step, but I still like to watch *Strictly Come Dancing* each week.

I guess I am saying this to warn people, parents and carers, who have similar intimidations around this art form. Because once I realised that I was allowed to like some poems and not like others, and that it didn't make me stupid, and once I realised that poetry gigs were no less intimidating than a comedy night (less so, because you are highly unlikely to be picked on) and once I realised that it was OK to change my mind about poems and poets, to change tastes as I read more or saw more or learnt more, and that it was as OK to read poems in books as it was to read them on Instagram or watch them in theatres as on Youtube, I could finally enjoy poetry again. And maybe stop paying to get into my own gigs.

Hollie McNish is a poet based between Cambridge and Glasgow. She has released three poetry collections – Papers, Cherry Pie *and* Plum *– and one poetic memoir,* Nobody Told Me, *for which she won the Ted Hughes Prize. She loves writing poems.*

How to encourage their reading

Children can't read all the time, but you can still keep up interest in all things bookish away from the page. In terms of literary accessories, the sky is the limit. There are temporary tattoos for children who like Antoine de Saint-Exupéry's *The Little Prince*, a shower curtain of Bilbo's front door in *The Hobbit*, a huge range of interesting bookcases and bookshelves, book-patterned wallpaper and Narnia-inspired candles.

There are also various trump card games with a literary angle, including *Once Upon A Time …* , which is based on characters in well-known fairy tales and features categories including bravery, wickedness, fashion sense and kissability. Older children may also enjoy my two packs of *The Writers Game* (one of modern authors, one of classic ones), where famous authors are pitted against each other for commercial success, critical acclaim, biopic factor and output. There are many more trump card games featuring everything from Shakespeare's plays to Greek myths, and for those who are as interested in the design of books as their content, Type Trumps focuses on individual typefaces, such as Helvetica and Futura, and their legibility or special powers.

Look out too for non-fiction card-based quiz games aimed at children, such as *History Heroes,* which tests children's knowledge of famous people such as Picasso, Tutankhamun, Joan of Arc and the Dalai Lama. If you're just after straightforward playing cards, the *Macmillan Alice Pack of Cards* is very attractive, featuring John Tenniel's original illustrations, while Prospero Art (prospero-art.com) produces a pack that also includes quotations from the books. There are of course more Harry Potter packs than you can shake a wand at.

A different kind of card game is based on the Victorian concept of a myriorama: a series of illustrated cards that can be rearranged in a number of combinations to form different stories. *The Ghost Story Box* is aimed at three- to five-year-olds and has twenty pieces for making up fairy stories, while *The Hollow Woods* is along similar lines but aimed at older children. Also for older children, *The*

Shadow World, with illustrations by the artist Shan Jiang, leads to more of a steampunk scenario. There are also dice-based versions of myrioramas, in which children roll dice with images on them and build up stories depending on how they land. These can also help in making up stories together and giving parents inspiration for bedtime tales.

Numerous games require playing around with words. Fridge-magnet words and letters have continued to be popular in our house well beyond schooldays. There are now various forms including ones dedicated to haiku, the moon and hedgehogs, as well as in various foreign languages. Also of interest is *Paint Chip Poetry*, which mixes colours and prompts to create poetry; another story prompter is *The Amazing Story Generator*, a flipbook of prompts that provides readers with a random mix of suggestions to use in creating their own unique story.

There are also jigsaw possibilities, among them the Bodleian Library in Oxford's *High Jinks* puzzles, which feature the highly illustrated covers of nineteenth-century children's books, especially those originally aimed at girls, while the *Ideal Bookshelf* puzzle, based on the artist Jane Mount's *Bibliophile* series, includes titles such as the *Book I Read Again and Again* and the *Book I Would Grab if the House is Burning*.

If your son or daughter is keen on making things, the *My Miniature Library* kit contains everything you need to make thirty tiny books (it's a cut, fold and glue make) as well as a bookcase for them: some are ready printed, others are blank so that your child can self-publish. On a larger scale, Zoe Toft discusses how she made her own temporary book den out of books for World Book Night on her excellent blog about children's books, playingbythebook.net.

READING HEROES

Although seeing friends and family reading helps encourage children to pick up a book themselves, famous role models can also foster a positive attitude to reading. The National Literacy Trust has done some excellent work over the last decade working with the Premier League and its footballers. The Premier League Primary Stars is a schools-based programme aimed at motivating children to improve their literacy levels, as is the Premier League Reading Stars – top-flight footballers from leading clubs in the UK pick their favourite books – and Writing Stars projects. Its poetry competition, co-judged by Rio Ferdinand, Olly Murs, Lauren Child and Joseph Coelho, attracted more than 25,000 entries. Around two-thirds of children who took part in the Reading Stars scheme say that seeing Premier League footballers reading and talking about books made them want to read more. More than half of them went on to visit a library as a result.

As well as advocating reading, some famous faces who are popular among children have also written books – indeed, whole series – for them. From the world of football there is Frank Lampard (*Frankie's Magic Football*) and Theo Walcott (T. J. series); from athletics, Jessica Ennis-Hill (*Evie's Magic Bracelet*); from dance, Darcey Bussell (*Magic Ballerina*); and from cycling, Chris Hoy (*Flying Fergus*). The *Kid Normal* books are written by BBC Radio 1 DJ Greg James and newsreader Chris Smith, and Steve Backshall's *The Falcon Chronicles* will appeal to anybody who enjoyed his adventure programmes on television.

LINKING INTERESTS TO BOOKS

As mentioned earlier, in the section on non-fiction, one way to interest your son or daughter in reading is to suggest books that link to their other hobbies. If they have particularly enjoyed the *Thor* films, that can be a great entry into Neil Gaiman's *Odd and the Frost Giants*, which is based on Norse mythology and the Vikings, and features all of the main characters from the films (for older children, Gaiman's *Norse Mythology* is also an excellent read). Another possibility would be *The Sleeping Army* by Francesca Simon, author of the Horrid Henry series, which is set in a parallel universe in which the Viking gods are still worshipped – this is also a good one for children who like chess, as the Lewis chessmen in the British Museum play an important part in the story.

Similarly, children who particularly like video games like *Fortnite* may find themselves drawn to books like *We See Everything* by William Sutcliffe, a dystopian thriller in a futuristic but still recognisable London, where there is constant drone surveillance and one of the lead adolescent characters has landed a dream job because of his gaming ability. Along the way it raises plenty of issues about family, love and ethics. For those more interested in coding than gaming, *The Thrilling Adventures of Lovelace and Babbage: The (Mostly) True Story of the First Computer* by Sydney Padua is a clever and funny steampunk graphic novel that follows the lives of the first computer programmers – Ada Lovelace (Lord Byron's daughter) and Charles Babbage – and riffs on what might have happened if their plans had come to fruition (they fight crime, they explore maths, they defeat bad spelling).

There are many possibilities when it comes to sport. For those interested in tennis, *Sisters and Champions: The True Story of Venus and Serena Williams* by Howard Bryant is an excellent introduction to the successful sisters, with an emphasis on following your dream whatever your childhood circumstances. For swimmers, *Splash* by Charli Howard follows a girl who aspires to swim in the Olympics. Again, alongside the sporting element, the book explores other themes, such as troublesome friend-ships and families, as well as body image.

Girls and boys who enjoy playing music will enjoy *Before John was a Jazz Giant: A Song of John Coltrane* by Carole Boston Weatherford, with illustrations by Sean Qualls, which focuses on the saxophonist's childhood and how the everyday sounds he heard around him as a young boy influenced his playing and composing. *My Museum* by Joanne Liu takes a similar, though this time wordless, approach to a visit to an art gallery by a small child who finds art not just in the exhibits, but everywhere, from other visitors' tattoos to the pattern of sunlight.

Children are also centre stage in *Kid Artists: True Tales of Childhood from Creative Legends*, written by David Stabler and illustrated by Doogie Horner. The young lives of a diverse collection of artists such as Vincent van Gogh, Georgia O'Keeffe and Beatrix Potter are detailed, and it does not shy away from including chal-lenging issues that faced those such as Jackson Pollock, who moved home many times and lost part of his index finger in an accident. A companion volume, *Kid Authors*, follows the same path, for writers such as J. K. Rowling and J. R. R. Tolkien. One for children who like both art and animals is *Frida Kahlo and her Animalitos*, written by Monica Brown and illustrated by John Parra, which concentrates on the animals (monkeys, birds, dogs and cats) that inspired the Mexican artist's colourful work.

BOOK GROUPS

In their book about running a successful book group, *Deconstructing Penguins: Parents, Kids, and the Bond of Reading*, Lawrence and Nancy Goldstone talk in depth about what books to choose. They argue strongly that rather than being satisfied with simply getting children to read anything at all, it *does* matter what titles children read, and they should be encouraged to read books that are challenging and well written, with careful plotting and intriguing characters. Their analogy is with eating: that your children should be eating healthy meals rather than junk food. Whatever you think of their approach, it's an excellent book for anybody who is thinking about starting a book group for children, with plenty of honest detail about their years of first-hand experience.

As with adult book groups, it's helpful to have some kind of structure and decide roughly what you'll be doing, but the key thing is not to be too rigid and let the children guide how the meetings unroll. You will want to start with a list of books to work through, so it's important to keep yourself up to date with what's out there and to ask around for suggestions too, but the children themselves will suggest other titles to go with your own thoughts.

Don't forget that libraries can be very helpful in ordering in multiple copies of the same title.

Some groups go for a book-by-book approach, choosing one or two individual titles per session, while others opt for a themed approach, or pick books shortlisted for awards, or by author, books that are favourites or books they haven't read yet. Ask the children what they would like to do, and make suggestions based on their interests as they emerge – although it is good  to gently ease them outside their comfort zone where possible. Mixing things up between fiction and non-fiction can be a good idea too, to stop it becoming a bit stale for all involved, and certainly don't forget graphic novels, picture books and poetry. Nor does it have to be all reading: drawing, writing or other book-related activities could all be included on an occasional basis. Once again, reading aloud is also well worth considering, as is acting out the plot of the book.

It's a good idea not to make it too much like a school lesson, so think carefully about the seating plan and keep it as comfortable and informal as possible (beanbags, if available, are a good option). Snacks and drinks will keep up energy levels and help make the experience fun, as will anything free, such as bookmarks. In terms of numbers, around ten is good, all roughly of the same age/ reading bracket. Meeting around once a month is not too frequent to put children off, but regular enough that they won't lose interest.

It is also worth contacting the authors of the books you are reading, even if it's just to say how much the children have enjoyed talking about their work. Most authors are great at replying to positive comments on Twitter or Instagram and that interaction will make the children's day.

In terms of how you structure the sessions, keeping it loose is a good way forward. As well as a general discussion of an individual title, you could try looking at just the beginnings and endings of various books. Or you could try some speed reading: give them a very limited amount of time to size up half a dozen books they've not previously read and then pick their favourite.

The Reading Agency runs Chatterbooks (chatterbooks. org.uk), the UK's largest network of children's reading groups in schools and libraries, as well as offering free resources to parents via their website, where there is also plenty of advice on how to run a reading club including lists of recommended books. Also worth investigating is the volunteer-run Federation of Children's Book Groups (fcbg.org.uk), which is aimed at parents as well as children. Local groups of adults around the country meet to talk about children's books and run speaker events as well as activities for children, including storytelling and author meet-ups. The CLPE has also set up book groups in schools and has a useful guide explaining how they did it on their website.

KEEP A BOOK LIST

Making a note of all the books you and your child read is a great idea. It's satisfying to see the titles rack up and it also provides useful talking points when you look back on which books have been read, perhaps comparing characters or plots in previous reads to current ones or realising that there are still books in a series or by a particular author that you meant to read but had forgotten about. Looking back on previously read books can also provide pleasant 'madeleine moment' links to when and where you read them, especially in years to come.

Your son or daughter could simply keep a numbered list of each book as they finish it (or decide not to continue with it), or add elements such as a rating out of ten, and even a few words of review. Older children who keep this kind of list might be interested in *My Life with Bob* by Pamela Paul, editor of the *New York Times Book Review*. It is an interesting memoir of her book list, a list of everything she's read since she was seventeen and what part it has played in her life.

A book list can also be revealing. As you and your child select books, you may not notice any patterns in your buying, but with a list you can look back and see if anything emerges. For example, it might reveal a heavy imbalance of male writers, which isn't always immediately noticeable, or highlight that after a long run of fiction it could be time for some poetry.

There is also the pleasure in owning your own book journal. Children like stationery and notebooks, so this is a good way to indulge them. Of course, any notebook is perfectly fine, but it's still nice to have a special private place in which to write. There are also online possibilities such as Goodreads and LibraryThing which do the same thing digitally.

BOOK COOKERY

Combining books and other activities is a great way to extend an interest in books. Cooking is one that particularly lends itself to exploring a book from a different angle. Naturally, there is a shelf of books and many pages online which offer to provide details about how to make the butterbeer in the Harry Potter series (*The Wizard's Cookbook* by Aurélia Beaupommier is strong on everything from Getafix's magic potion in the Asterix books to the optimistic invisibility potion from *Dungeons and Dragons*). But some cookery books can take you deeper into the story.

Moomins Cookbook, based on Tove Jansson's beloved Moomin characters, is subtitled *An Introduction to Finnish Cookery* and provides exactly that, with appropriate extracts and illustrations of the main characters preparing and eating food. *The Secret Garden Cookbook* by Amy Cotler not only features recipes inspired by Frances Hodgson Burnett's classic story published in 1910, but also focuses on food history around that period, how typical menus varied between classes, regional cookery (especially in Yorkshire) and dishes the lead character Mary would have eaten in India.

A good compendium of recipes from various books is *The Little Library Cookbook* by Kate Young, which includes instructions for how to make your own green eggs and ham, as well as *tunna pannkakor* or Swedish pancakes for those who enjoy Astrid Lindgren's Pippi Longstocking stories. Some of the recipes can also be found online at Young's site The Little Library Café (thelittlelibrarycafe. com). Also look out for *The Great British Bake Off* winner

Nadiya Hussain's *Bake Me a Story*, which weaves stories and recipes together, and her separate Christmas-themed volume.

In all of Enid Blyton's *Famous Five* books, Julian, Dick, Anne, George and Timmy enjoy their food, especially frequent picnics. It would be easy to follow their lead as your child reads the appropriate book – this would mean lettuce and Spam, sardines, and cucumber dipped in vinegar (*Five Go Off to Camp*); ham (*Five on a Secret Trail*); and potted meat (*Five on Kirrin Island Again*). Two specialist cookbooks recreate the Five's picnics and other meals: *Five Go Feasting: Famously Good Recipes* by Josh Sutton, and *Jolly Good Food* by Allegra McEvedy, which includes other Blyton favourites such as *The Folk of the Faraway Tree* and the *Malory Towers* series. Again, make sure to use newer, revised editions to avoid problematic themes and language. For more cookery books and books about food, see the CLPE's dedicated list of suggestions from p. 194.

Older children who have read Gerald Durrell's *My Family and Other Animals*, about his early life on Corfu, may also enjoy *Dining with the Durrells* by David Shimwell. The book features Gerald's mother Louisa's recipes from the Durrell archive at Jersey Zoo, not only for cakes and scones, but also for chicken curry and Corfiot fish stew, with an interesting selection reflecting Louisa's Indian upbringing.

Tips

Book allowance: if you give your children pocket money, consider ring-fencing a portion of it to go towards buying books or, if you can, adding a little extra to what they normally receive but earmarked for book-buying.

If you have space, create a comfortable reading nook somewhere in the house, maybe in your child's bedroom, which is a special place where they can settle down with a good book. A search for 'children's reading nook' on Pinterest will reveal plenty of ideas.

A book-themed fashion industry has sprung up in the last few years, so look out for your children's favourite characters – on T-shirts, hoodies, earrings, hats and other accessories – for birthday and Christmas presents. (To be honest, this is also one for grown-ups: I wear my *Harry the Dirty Dog* and *Mike Mulligan and his Steam Shovel* T-shirts with pride and have got through more Tintin T-shirts than I care to count).

The Literary Gift Company has a good range (theliterarygiftcompany.com) as does the Literary Emporium (literaryemporium.co.uk) and Etsy.com.

Consider suggesting to your children that they write fan fiction about their favourite characters and worlds, adding their own imagination to what they've read. Meg Cabot is among famous writers who have done this, in her case *Star Wars*-based fan fiction when she was a teenager. There is a huge online world of fan fiction sites, although these need to be carefully researched as a lot of content is not age-appropriate for youngsters.

Do encourage your children to read in languages other than English, whether there is a bilingual aspect to your household or not. I remember enjoying reading *Winnie-the-Pooh* in Latin and Asterix stories in French at school, and have enjoyed reading *Miffy* in Spanish to my children. Mantra Lingua (mantralingua.com) is particularly good at producing dual-language books for bilingual children and families, or indeed for those who simply want to learn a new language, as well as tactile titles for those who are visually impaired.

After being a secondary school English teacher for over a decade, I have learned some of the essential ingredients that combine to make young people who are fit to face the challenges of twenty-first-century life. In my experience, reading is an essential way to guide and support young people on their road to adulthood.

If you've ever sat facing a teacher at a school parents' evening, you'll no doubt have been told that your child needs to 'read more'. This isn't just a maxim used (and over-used) by teachers: there is basis for this recommendation in numerous studies conducted worldwide. The bottom line is that reading is good fun. Who doesn't love being transported into a different world to live a different life for a little while?

To encourage reading that supports your child's academic studies, you could request reading lists from your child's school, or use the school's website to look at your child's proposed curriculum and see what sort of topics they are set to study, then use a website like goodreads.com to find books that cover similar topics. If children already have a point of reference when learning new material, it is more likely to be understood. As your child gets older, they will be studying set texts for their exams, so why not read these texts too? You could even ask the school to lend you a copy to read (and enjoy the stunned look on the teacher's face as you request it!). The complexity of exam preparation can be quite isolating for parents, especially when they are keen to support their child through this testing time; having knowledge of the subject matter or set texts could really help to break some of these barriers and allow you to play your part at this crucial time in their academic career.

The key thing is interest: show your curiosity about whatever your child is learning or reading. You are not expected to constantly be the expert or even have all of the answers but *be interested*. Show that you're keen to learn something new and that you're not afraid to be challenged to go out of your comfort zone. You'll be amazed at the impact this has on the development of young minds.

When you feel the time is appropriate, talk about the book that your child is reading. Meal times provide an ideal opportunity to do this. Simple questions like 'What are you reading at the moment?' can encourage young people to talk about their reading experiences and start the conversation.

If you are reading with your child, here are a series of adapted prompts you can use to support their understanding and thinking about a text. It's important here to have a conversation *with* your child rather than talking *to* your child. Instead of putting pressure on yourself to think up specifics, keep the questions open and create a dialogue.

Why do you think (insert name of character) did that/ acted in that way?

What do you notice about what is happening here? Can you tell me what has happened?

If you could ask the character/author a question, what would it be? What would you like to find out?

What does this make you think/feel?

What do you think might happen next?

Does anything in the book remind you of anything that has happened to you?

Do you feel sorry for the characters? Happy for them?

Do you know how they feel?

Were there any words in that section you didn't understand? Can we work out what they might mean?

Have you read or come across anything similar to this elsewhere? When?

A useful prompt to ask your child following any answer is 'What makes you say that?'. This question forces your child to justify and provide evidence of their thinking which, in turn, further strengthens their understanding.

Some texts you read may prompt interesting moral debates that you can chew over as a family. These can be managed using a simple Visible Thinking Routine. Visible Thinking Routines (or VTRs) were developed using the research of Ron Ritchhart and Harvard University Project Zero and are used in schools internationally to support young people's habits of thinking about anything, not just reading. If setting up a debate, make it clear that only one person should speak at a time and that the next response either needs to agree with, build on or challenge the previous point. For example:

'I'd like to agree with Mum's view/Dad's view because
    I think ...'

'I'm going to build on what _____ said because I
    think ...'

'I'd like to challenge _____' s point about ...'

Be strict with the wording of each response and you'll
soon have young debaters who can agree or disagree
with each other in a purposeful and orderly fashion.
Turning reading material into a debate helps the child
to see the relevance of the story or subject matter,
outside of the text they are reading. It makes their
reading pertinent and current.

*Tracy Goodyear is Head of English at King Edward VI
Handsworth School for Girls in Birmingham and Founding
Fellow for the Chartered College of Teaching.*

Sounds and pictures
Enjoying the varieties of reading

PICTURE BOOKS

If you ever need an example of why picture books are such an ideal introduction to the delights of reading, you simply need to watch a small child reading a picture book by themselves and see how much they are enthralled by it, how they move backwards and forwards through the book, how attentively they examine the pictures, and how they will probably start reading the book again as soon as they finish it. The earlier your child learns that reading is enjoyable, the more likely they are to continue reading as they grow older.

Picture books play an important role in children's literature and do not simply provide a step on the route to chapter books. They help budding readers learn the basic mechanics of reading a book as well as teaching narrative structure, how to read between the lines, how to use additional story material shown in the pictures but not stated in the text to understand what is happening, and how to empathise with the characters. Poet and former Children's Laureate Michael Rosen argues that this is much more than simple inference: 'It's interpretation, cognition, logic, symbolism, holding several ideas in the head at the same time, the germs of abstract thought through analogy.'

Picture books allow children to see the world as the writer and illustrator see it, and, in fact, to step inside their world. Indeed, the CLPE's Power of Pictures project, designed to focus on the development of visual literacy skills in primary-aged children, encourages an appreciation of the key role of picture books and graphic texts in developing children's comprehension and critical reading skills at all ages and stages, and on the use of illustration as a tool for developing and communicating ideas. Their Power of Pictures website (clpe.org.uk/ powerofpictures) contains recommendations for picture books that can be used with children across the primary years, and introduces children to the role of authors and illustrators through a series of videos of published author/illustrators reading their picture books aloud, sharing how they illustrate characters and talking about themselves and how they create picture book texts.

Visual literacy is also an important skill and one that can easily be overlooked, but which mirrors the same kind of processes as those developed by reading chapter books and poetry, and is particularly useful for reluctant or struggling readers. Pictures help young readers analyse a story. Reading is not always about building vocabulary.

Most importantly, picture books make reading fun. Children love art and the images draw the children in as well as imparting meaning. One beauty of picture books is that they cover so many subjects and celebrate important principles such as friendship, self-expression and bravery, important elements of a positive moral compass and behavioural development. Children can easily empathise with a small bear who is unhappy. Picture books certainly provide a good way of starting a conversation about delicate topics such as bullying, a new sibling, divorce or dementia. The pictures can help to make potentially upsetting issues – such as getting to grips with trying new foods – less overwhelming and more accessible. Of course, you can still read aloud a wordless picture book, because it gives you a blank canvas for you and your child to improvise around. Neither of you can get it wrong.

Children reread books constantly and picture books are certainly no exception; indeed they are usually written with the idea of rereading to the fore, often with rhymes that lend themselves to being repeated out loud and give children the pleasure of anticipating what line is coming next. Most adults, when asked to name favourite childhood books, will come up with several picture book suggestions, which shows how deeply they affect us. Don't hurry your children away from them when they are delighted to read them – picture books are not a type of reading to 'move on from', but are important reading at all stages, and it's important not to make children feel bad about something they should be enjoying.

COMICS

Comics are bright and colourful, often very funny and engaging, not too long and simply a lot of fun. From a selfish point of view, I also enjoyed the nostalgic rush of digging out saved boxes of back issues of *Whizzer and Chips*, *Tiger and Scorcher*, *Dandy*, *Beano*, plus the occasional *Beezer*, from the loft and looking at them with my own children.

One reason comics are still so popular is that the subject matter is close to children's hearts. As well as moving along at a cracking rate, they focus on characters to whom your children can easily relate or aspire. And while there is still the same issue with a lack of BAME characters as in other areas of children's publishing, this is hopefully starting to change, with the Pakistani-American character Ms Marvel now rumoured to be heading towards the big screen, having already won a prestigious Hugo Award for its first collection by G. Willow Wilson (writer), Adrian Alphona (artist) and Jake Wyatt (artist).

As with all other kinds of reading, be prepared for comics to be reread continually. My old ones, even the much older ones like *Eagle* annuals, have visibly undergone a second bout of heavy reading. We kept a box of *Beano* comics in our boys' rooms, and while they were regularly topped up with newer additions and the occasional summer special, the older ones were just as fondly reread.

Sadly, traditional comics have seen a marked decline over the last few decades and the likes of *Whizzer and Chips* have been replaced by magazines that tie in to children's TV programmes, films or toys, usually with no comics content. The *Beano* is the last one left that adults will remember with fondness, but there are some exceptions such as the *Doctor Who Magazine*, which always has a comic strip, and the excellent newcomer the *Phoenix*, which publishes original, advert-free comic content on a mainly subscription basis.

A great thing about comics is that they can be picked up and put down quickly and easily. While they can be something of a bridge between reading picture books and text-heavy chapter books, there should be no hard and fast rules about when (if indeed ever) comic reading should be phased out. I remember one of my sons reading a *Bash Street Kids* annual at the same time as Philip Pullman's *His Dark Materials* trilogy. It didn't seem at all strange to him to have both of them on the go at the same time.

GRAPHIC NOVELS

There is no very definite separation between comics and graphic novels, although the latter are certainly more than just stretched-out comics or the adventures of superheroes (though there's nothing wrong with either of those).

If you are worried about how beneficial graphic novels are for your child's reading, take a look at a selection. There are of course some wordless graphic novels, but in general they have plenty of text to read. Yes, there are lots of illustrations and drawings, but these are books that still need traditional reading skills to enjoy them. Moreover, images have become an increasingly key part in our society with the rise of social media, so younger readers readily relate to and are drawn towards them.

Certainly you shouldn't make your child feel that it is embarrassing to read a graphic novel; it's really not. Their friends won't make that kind of judgement and neither should you. Graphic novels should be approached as 'legitimate' reading material, just as 'serious' as non-graphic ones. It's worth remembering why you want your child to read. Reading is only a means to an end, and reading a graphic novel develops the same kind of skills as reading a non-graphic one. As Neil Gaiman said in his 2013 Reading Agency lecture, 'the idea that they foster illiteracy is tosh'.

The key thing that graphic novels do is engage the reader directly. This is particularly important if your child does not enjoy more traditional books, or if they are just starting to read. This starts immediately with the covers, which tend to be extremely well designed and which pull the prospective reader in even before they've opened the book. As they pick it up and flick through, it doesn't feel oppressive: it looks like it could be achievable. For an older child, they appeal because they look mature, not childish, and are likely to contain something suitable for them in terms of subject matter. While both picture books and graphic novels can appeal to readerships of all ages, graphic novels often (though not always) succeed better at appealing to older children.

The combination of words and images helps to propel children through books where a more dense text-only version might slow them down and even overwhelm and defeat them. Boredom and frustration are not generally qualities associated with graphic novels, which tend to be fast paced.

Graphic novels are also as gripping as a 'traditional' novel. They have exciting plots, include cliffhangers, pose moral questions, provide character development and surge towards the finale. They also tend towards high-quality text. The only difference is that they have visuals alongside the text, which help to reinforce it – if your child enjoys what they're reading, it's likely they'll go back to reread and gain a deeper understanding of the story. It's important to remember that there are different kinds of learners: visual learners will be encouraged by a graphic novel and this confidence will also reassure them that they can deal with text, where they may otherwise be put off by a long paragraph or extended description. Images provide hints to meanings where words might not be of help. Indeed, sometimes a visual is better since it leaves the reader to use their imagination to consider the motivation of a character. One piece of advice given to writers is often 'show, don't tell', and graphic novels are ideally placed to do just this, getting readers right into the story.

One of the qualities that reading develops is empathy. This can be particularly true with graphic novels, where emotions and sensations are presented visually and clearly. Similarly, readers of graphic novels learn to infer as they read from what is not actually spelled out in the text, the panels of the story being necessarily fragmentary and leaving plenty to the imagination – again, this is where the 'show, don't tell' element comes into play (as it does with any comic strip such as Charles Schulz's *Peanuts* or *Calvin and Hobbes*).

If a child finds books challenging, there is a considerable sense of achievement when they finish a graphic novel compared to the feeling of failure with other books. This is not to be underestimated. Being able to add a notch to your reading tally is a pleasure for all ages, a boasting opportunity, and creates a feeling that reading can be not only achievable but also enjoyable, while at the same time building up their reading stamina.

Graphic novels can also be good books to read aloud to your child. I enjoyed reading the Tintin stories to mine, pointing at the frames and reading the text as we moved along, allowing them enough time to digest the images without (hopefully) slowing down the pace of the narrative. They then went back to the books regularly and looked at them on their own, well before they could fully understand the text, and then again when they could read it themselves with the occasional nudge for the harder vocabulary.

In any event, there's simply no need to choose between two styles of book: variety is the spice of life, especially when it comes to reading. I remember reading Tintin at the same time as *The Children of Green Knowe* by Lucy M. Boston, and have come back to his adventures regularly throughout my adult life for a relaxing (and admittedly nostalgic) read, each time coming across something I'd missed before in Hergé's complex universe – if I'm honest, I've come back to them more than the Green Knowe series. When I was in my teens, I read these books in French, which improved my vocabulary considerably in very enjoyable circumstances (I admit less success with Asterix translated into Latin but I did enjoy *Winnie-the-Pooh* as *Winnie Ille Pu* in translation). I would be very sad to see Tintin go. There are also halfway-house series, such as Jeff Kinney's *Diary of a Wimpy Kid* and Jonathan Meres' *The World of Norm*, which mix large amounts of illustration with lively text.

As with other books it's important to choose age-appropriate titles in the same way that you'd pick traditional ones, as well as trying to make the choice as diverse as you would with any other type of book selection in terms of gender and race. For older YA readers, *American Born Chinese* by Gene Luen Yang, which looks at questions of identity and integration, has been hugely popular. Also worth considering is *Illegal* by Eoin Colfer and Andrew Donkin, illustrated by Giovanni Rigano, which tells the story of a child migrant from

Africa to Europe. Look out too for the darkly dystopian *Dark Satanic Mills*, written by popular YA author Marcus Sedgwick and his brother Julian, with illustrations by John Higgins. Brian Selznick has written a couple of intriguing graphic novel hybrids that mix extensive illustrations with text: *The Marvels* and *The Invention of Hugo Cabret*.

There are also graphic novel versions of already printed books – such as Philippa Pearce's *Tom's Midnight Garden*, Rick Riordan's Percy Jackson books or Eoin Colfer's Artemis Fowl series, not to mention Philip Pullman's *His Dark Materials* trilogy – and you may find that your child enjoys revisiting the original story but in this different format. Alternatively, they may have heard them as an audiobook and want to try it out in 'traditional' book format. And there are graphic versions of classics such as Shakespeare's plays and the *Odyssey*; these can be wonderful ways of grappling with key works of literature, and since teachers use films as one way into set texts at school, graphic novel versions hardly seem like a jump into the unknown.

One side effect of reading graphic novels is that your children may well be inspired to try their hand at producing one themselves: a great way of understanding how characterisation and plot are constructed, as well as developing their own artistic skills.

An interview

WITH CHARLIE ADLARD, UK COMICS LAUREATE 2017–19, AND HANNAH BERRY, UK COMICS LAUREATE 2019–21

Were you encouraged to read comics as a child?

CA: My parents never *discouraged* me, that's for sure. I read books too, so perhaps for them if I was reading 'serious' literature then the other stuff was fine. Also, I presume since I was drawing comics and showed a talent for it at such an early age, they might have realised that reading comics might've provided me with that little bit of extra inspiration.

HB: I was: my mother read comics from a very young age – in fact they helped her learn English as a young Spanish-speaker in the USA – so they were always on our shelves. *Calvin and Hobbes* was a particular family favourite.

What do comics/graphic fiction offer readers that they can't get elsewhere?

CA: I think it's just another form of entertainment. Subject-wise, I don't think they

offer anything else over and beyond any other source. Comics are a medium, *not* a genre, so they should be treated as such, in all forms. If someone wants to read comics over books, then fine, it's a choice of medium. Similar to someone electing to watch a film over listening to music, it's just a different experience. But equally valid.

HB: It might surprise people who are not used to the medium to learn the incredible levels of subtlety you can get from a comic. The visual elements provide a huge amount of context, some of it subconsciously, and the combination of text and image often yields a more tacit layer of understanding. The best part is that all this context is readily available to most readers from any age and of any reading ability, as visual literacy is pretty much innate. It's a very exciting medium to work in, I can tell you.

People tend to think that they're especially appropriate for boys, but that seems strange to me and I don't see why girls can't enjoy them too.

HB: Comics are for everyone, and anyone who says otherwise needs a stern talking to.

CA: I completely agree. I think though, in the past, the genre has been dominated by supposedly male-dominated themes – whether it's war, action or superheroes – with the majority of creators and publishers being male. This is slowly changing. And why can't female readers enjoy action, if they want? Similarly, why can't male readers enjoy a non-genre drama or a romance, for instance? Japan and France have a more broad audience for their material. This is definitely something ingrained in our culture, which does need to change.

Are there any dos and don'ts for parents?

CA: No more advice other than what you would do as a parent in an ordinary bookshop ... to review the material before purchasing. All the obvious stuff. I'd advise them to seek out, shall we say, the more non-populist stores, if they can. The ones that treat comics *as* a medium and not as a way of selling the latest Marvel movie tie-in, for example. Page 45 in Nottingham, for instance, lays its content out as a bookstore, has knowledgeable staff (for the beginners) and feels a welcoming, inclusive place. That's the way comic shops should go.

HB: I'd recommend finding comics that match their children's interests: there's so much choice out there that you're sure to find something for even the pickiest reader. You could take them into a comic shop and let them browse, and if you need pointers then the staff will usually be happy (if not outright delighted) to help. There are some great shops all around the country, though Gosh! Comics in London, Page 45 in Nottingham and Dave's Comics in Brighton are the three that I know best, and all have fully stocked shelves for younger readers. In fact, Page 45 has a section on their website where you can fill in your interests and they will send you tailor-made recommendations.

AUDiOBOOKS

Sales of audiobooks are booming, thanks in part to the increasing popularity of podcasts making audio in general a popular medium. In the UK in 2018 sales were up 43 per cent, to £69 million, with the largest share of the pie belonging to Amazon's Audible provider. It's the same all over the world: China's latest reading report reveals that more than a quarter of Chinese people under eighteen listened to audiobooks in 2018.

One of the major advantages of audiobooks is that you can enjoy them while you're doing something else. Like many people, I found that the best way of soothing my boys during a long car journey was to let them listen to one of their favourite stories. We went through the whole Roald Dahl catalogue a couple of times, *Atticus the Storyteller* by Lucy Coats (ditto — and which also led to our youngest asking for the book and reading it for himself), a couple of *How to Train Your Dragon* books from the sequence by Cressida Cowell (really marvellously read by David Tennant), *Stig of the Dump* by Clive King (surprisingly this wasn't a success, even though read nicely by Tony Robinson) and a host of David Walliams's books, read by the author. The impact on the car noise/irritation levels was immediate, remarkable and sustained. But of course they're not just for the car: your children can listen to audiobooks in small chunks at any time, including of course at bedtime.

In the same way that reading graphic novels can lead to children making up their own stories, so too can they produce their own homemade versions of favourite stories or ones they've written themselves, particularly useful if they fall into the kinaesthetic learning category (learning by doing) as well as the auditory one. And just like reading traditional books, there's nothing to stop your children listening to them again and again (our *Atticus the Storyteller* CDs saw some serious replay action).

Audiobooks certainly provide a deep experience. As well as the expressive readings, there is also scope for a musical soundtrack and sound effects. As a child I enjoyed the Rev. W. Awdry's railway series, but Johnny Morris's recordings on vinyl added so much more to my experience, especially as his Thomas sounded very like a small child. Another early favourite was *Winnie-the-Pooh*, which came with a book so I could follow along as the narrator read the story, with chimes to indicate when to turn the page. Indeed, research indicates that following the text of a story while listening helps to develop word recognition and reading ability.

I loved reading *The Lord of the Rings* when I was bit older, but I couldn't believe my luck when, just after I had finished, in 1981, the BBC produced a radio series, which I lapped up (for me, Michael Hordern and John Le Mesurier are Gandalf and Bilbo, not Ian McKellen and Ian Holm or Martin Freeman). It had the most tremendous soundtrack by Stephen Oliver, which is playing in the background as I write these words. I learnt the songs from the books by listening and relistening. For Tolkien fans I would also strongly recommend hunting down Nicol Williamson's reading of the book from 1974, in which he voiced all the roles himself.

Audiobooks also naturally form part of a reading-aloud childhood. While it's generally a better experience for children if there's a live narrator next to them, audiobooks provide an excellent alternative, with the added benefit to the listener that the narrator doesn't try to skip bits or sound a little bored on repeated readings. They also offer the chance to hear a range of accents and dialects from around the UK and indeed from around the world. This is valuable in broadening a child's worldview as well as maybe offering a familiar voice with which they can identify.

As with graphic novels (which themselves are now being turned into audiobooks), audiobooks are part of a general literary childhood, and should certainly not be seen as some kind of fraudulent replacement for a hard-back in the hand. Storytelling, after all, is far older than reading a printed book, and audio simply offers an alternative route into building vocabulary and all the other skills that help make your child confident with words. Listening to the spoken word exposes them to the rhythm and patterns of speech that could be overlooked while reading, as well as allowing the opportunity to offer them elements that can make the story come alive in a more personal way, for example through the use of authentic accents or well-timed humour.

Audiobooks are very accessible, and for a child who is finding it hard getting to grips with a printed book, audiobooks can help them to enjoy a story, with the added benefit that it could be beyond their reading level. Rather than stopping and starting and failing to really get into a story, an audiobook keeps the pace up and is continually entertaining. Interestingly, research shows that we're less likely to give up on listening to an audiobook than reading a book.

An audiobook can also add meaning to the text through prosody: the way the words are spoken, the intonation, the pace and the elements of stress or irony that are brought out in a way that is impossible in a traditional book. This can be particularly helpful with texts such as Shakespeare's plays, in which the meanings of

Case study: Will Evans

Will is the son of a friend of mine; I knew that he had found reading a challenge as a boy and asked him to explain his own journey in books.

'Torak woke with a jolt from a sleep he had never meant to have.' I will never forget these words, the first words of the first proper book I ever read by myself.

But it wasn't the first time I had heard them. Growing up with dyslexia meant that I found it very hard to read by myself. As a solution to this, when I was eight, I tried audiobooks, the first of which was *Wolf Brother* by Michelle Paver, read by Sir Ian McKellen. This sparked an interest in me for fantasy. Soon I started to pick up books myself, again starting with *Wolf Brother*, then going on to read titles such as the Skulduggery Pleasant series, *The Hobbit*, *Eragon* and other fantasy epics. Although some were quite long, they were mostly on the fairly light side and not immensely difficult to read. That was until I started reading George R. R. Martin's *A Song of Ice and Fire*, the books on which the *Game of Thrones* television series is based.

Two things were evident when I started reading the first book. One, I was going to love this series: it had such a vivid and detailed world that it was right up my street. And two, I might never actually finish it. It took me several months to get even 20 per cent of the way through the book, and I was starting to lose interest. It was at this moment that I reached for the audiobook version. In the same way that they had helped me get over my hurdle when I was learning to read, audiobooks were able to help me get over this hurdle again as an adult.

Looking back now that I'm twenty and studying mechanical engineering at the University of Bath, I can see that the audiobooks took away the difficulty that I was having with reading and allowed me to enjoy the stories that were being told, allowed me to keep track of what was going on rather than trying to keep track of where the words were on the page. Even though I am now a person who reads more books than I listen to, I strongly support audiobooks as they were the tool I used at the beginning of my reading journey, the most difficult part, to break down my own barriers and jump into these amazing worlds to fully grasp the enjoyment of reading.

ambiguous words or phrases are often made clearer when heard spoken by a good narrator. According to a study by University College London (though admittedly commissioned by Audible), audiobook users actually enjoy a deeper and more emotional experience by listening to a story read to them than by watching films or television. Mark Haddon, author of *The Curious Incident of the Dog in the Night-Time*, has even said that he doesn't feel that he has read a book properly until he's had it read to him.

On the downside, research suggests that we tend to miss some subtleties when listening to an audiobook and that reading print is still the way to gain deep understanding of texts. But that does not mean that listening to audiobooks is pointless; it is simply a different way of enjoying books and should still be encouraged.

FINDING AUDIOBOOKS

Listening Books (listening-books.org.uk) is a UK charity with a huge library of fiction and non-fiction audiobooks available for both children and adults who have difficulty reading or holding a book, through the post on CD, or by download or online streaming.

The biggest commercial player in the audiobook market is Audible, owned by Amazon, while Google has also joined the market via its Google Play Store. There are various other possibilities online, including iTunes,

Naxos AudioBooks and buying direct from booksellers and publishers. But there are many places to find alternatives on CD, vinyl (especially in second-hand shops – I've been looking for Alan Garner's readings of his *Stone Book Quartet* for years and am still hopeful!) and online.

Libraries, of course, are perfect places to find audiobooks, and many are experimenting with new ideas such as special reading rooms for children's audiobooks and tailored tablets to borrow e-books, audiobooks and magazines.

Technology is also bringing us new ways of listening to audiobooks. Amazon's Alexa devices now offer *Choose Your Own Adventure* audiobooks. Along the same lines as the *Choose Your Own Adventure* titles and *Fighting Fantasy* single role-playing books by Steve Jackson and Ian Livingstone that were huge hits in the 1980s (my copy of *The Warlock of Firetop Mountain* has proved popular for two generations), listeners are asked to make decisions at various points in the narrative which take them down different pathways.

DIGITAL READING

The way we read has been changing this century, shrinking books and indeed entire libraries onto pocket-sized electronic devices as mobile apps and digital technology bring reading to a wired generation.

National Literacy Trust research suggests that the number of children and young people aged between nine and eighteen who are reading digitally is rising, and that twice as many who read above the level expected for their age read fiction both in print and on screen. Its figures show that one in five read both fiction and non-fiction entirely on screens.

On the other hand, a survey by the Reading Agency for World Book Night also indicates that smartphone usage gets in the way of reading, with 72 per cent of young people acknowledging that the time they spend checking their phone cuts into their reading time.

Announcing the survey's results, Debbie Hicks, Creative Director at the Reading Agency, said: 'Smartphones can help us connect with others and learn more about the world around us. But this survey shows that many of us struggle to switch off and that this can take a toll on our wellbeing. Reading is the perfect way to disconnect. This doesn't mean abandoning your smartphone – there are lots of brilliant audiobooks and e-books that can help you escape into another world.'

It is a tricky subject, as many parents will be keen to see their children spending less rather than more time on their screens. Interestingly, the *Print Matters* report by the major UK children's publisher Egmont indicates that reading printed books with your child is more of an emotional experience than using a screen because of the physical nature of snuggling up together to read, especially at times of the year that are traditionally special for families, such as Christmas, but that e-books and apps work well when your child is reading alone. Here's what the report says:

> The physical book prompts bonding and cuddling. Touching and turning the pages together is enjoyed by both parents and children. Parents find passing the book around is good when reading to more than one child. Larger formats and plenty of illustrations allow for better sharing, and this is especially true for younger children.

What you certainly should not do is confiscate electronic items and attempt to force your children to read a book you plonk down in front of them. Associating reading with punishment is a poor idea.

Unicorns, Almost

A different kind of audiobook

'A dynamic working museum that celebrates the ongoing story of books.' That's how Emma Balch describes The Story of Books, based in the book town of Hay-on-Wye, which she set up in 2018. Its first major project is *Unicorns, Almost* (unicornsalmost.com), a play by Owen Sheers about the life and work of the Second World War poet Keith Douglas.

'It's the first truly immersive audiobook,' explains Emma. 'The one-man play by Dan Krikler is superb, but obviously text-heavy, and what I wanted to do was to provide a guide to Douglas's particular situation. So what we did is create a theatrical world designed for a communal listening experience. We mixed a dramatic reading by an actor with music and sound effects to create a fifty-five-minute soundscape. This is played in the setting of an evocative, immersive set, full of objects and books linked to Douglas, which makes for a powerful shared listening experience.'

The result is a variation on listening to an audiobook. 'There is an element of it being a communal experience, with people looking at the set as they listen to the audio and finding connections in that way, but we also noticed some people sitting by themselves to concentrate on the words or even simply just closing their eyes,' says Emma.

'It's been a great success and I think it shows that there are alternatives to accessing older works than simply republishing them as a book. By retelling the story in a fresh way, it can help to reach new audiences.'

All young children love books, partly because they open a window to their imagination, and partly because they share the experience with grown-ups they love. Young readers, or audiences at that age, enjoy almost any story, especially if it comes from people they love and spend time with. Not all young children get to experience books, however. For many they are a luxury easily replaced by a screen. Moreover, fewer children of colour or from minority cultural backgrounds get to see themselves in a story. There are many reasons for this, and they have been covered in several reports over the years, most recently the CLPE Reflecting Realities report and the Booktrust Represents reports.

What makes a good book for young children? For a start it has to be attractive, or at least interesting, to adults, too, because they are going to share the story at some stage; and if it's a hit, they will share it over and over again. The more often the book is read, the more chances the child has to absorb the story, its nuances and playfulness. This builds their confidence, verbal skills and reasoning ability.

Next, the book should represent the world as it should be, rather than as it is. That means adding equality, balance and wonder into the mix – blended with fun, of course! Some stories offer adults a chance to include these things in a discussion, others embed them in their plots or characters. It is wonderful to see such acceptance, empathy and joy come from young children experiencing simple things or working things out for themselves.

Whether or not to include illustrations is a subjective choice, but it should be noted that most children are able to 'read' pictures, even complex ones, especially when they are well matched with the text. This reinforces the wonder of children's picture books, where words and pictures combine to make the experience of a book memorable.

Finally, the book should have a tactile quality because young children also learn by feeling, smelling or even tasting the pages. All of these experiences

become memories, which – more often than not –
create more book lovers, readers and creators. Aren't
books great?

*Zimbabwean-born Ken Wilson-Max is publisher at Alanna
Max Books. He illustrates, writes and designs books for very
young children, including* Where's Lenny?, Lenny and
Wilbur *and* Astrogirl.

How to maintain interest
Getting out and about

LIBRARIES

Public libraries in the UK are surviving in the face of severe underfunding, with ongoing closures and reduced staffing levels. Nevertheless, librarians are still working hard and imaginatively to provide plenty of reading opportunities for you and your children, so it still very much makes sense to join your local library. With their own library card, your child suddenly has an almost endless choice of books to try out, however old they are.

The beauty of the library system is that they can follow whatever reading path they choose. I remember that when I was small I always went with my parents to the library on a Thursday evening after tea (it was the same small market town library in which the poet Philip Larkin first cut his teeth as a librarian). We handed back the books we'd taken out the previous week – or at least those we had finished or in which we'd lost interest – and then my parents would simply let me wander off and explore. I flitted about all over the place, mostly of course in the children's section, but also in other areas in the books earmarked for grown-ups. After about half an hour I'd have picked up an armful of books, basically anything that caught my eye. Over the next week, I'd only read one or two at most, flick through another couple and probably didn't even open the others. But it didn't matter as I could hang on to whatever books I fancied and take back any I didn't. And nobody judged me. And it was free. I remember in particular picking out from the library shelves the *Littlenose* stories about a Stone Age schoolboy, written by John Grant, after listening to him narrating them on the BBC's *Jackanory*, which is where I first heard them. It's never too early to start showing your children that their local library is a marvellous place to spend time.

Try not to be in a rush when you go to the library with your children. It should be a relaxing experience and one without any pressure about choosing the 'right' book. Libraries also put on plenty of events so if you give yourself plenty of time for your library visit, you might coincide with an activity, a craft session or an author reading. When my eldest two were very small indeed, they accidentally crawled through a bookcase partition into a reading by Michael Morpurgo at our local library, for much older children, but he very kindly made them welcome. I'm not sure how much it improved their literacy levels, but it certainly gave the library an added sense of glamour for them for future visits.

If you don't have a lot of space at home for books, using a library is doubly good because you can keep rotating volumes while at the same time always having something children are interested in reading at home.

Also encourage your children to make as much use as they can of their school library, if they are lucky enough to have one. Although there are no official figures about how many school libraries there are in the UK, statistics from the National Literacy Trust indicate that they can be hugely helpful in motivating children to enjoy reading and in improving their overall levels of literacy, maths and science attainment.

One of the best things to sign your child up to is the Summer Reading Challenge, which is run by the Reading

Agency every year in partnership with public libraries throughout the UK: around 700,000 children aged four to eleven take part. Children are encouraged to choose and read six books during the summer holidays, a time when reading skills can fall away. They get various rewards for every book they finish (there is a different theme each year) and a certificate at the end. The dedicated website (summerreadingchallenge.org.uk) has plenty of book recommendations, videos and competitions to add to the fun.

Other library-run reading schemes include Bookbug's Library Challenge in Scotland, run by the Scottish Book Trust (scottishbooktrust.com), which encourages children of any age to borrow books regularly from their local library and win certificates, as they collect special stamps each time they read a book.

Of course, you should make use of the knowledgeable librarians themselves. They are always more than happy to help and suggest titles.

VISITS

If your child particularly loves a book or series of books, it's quite possible that there will be locations linked to the stories that you can visit which really bring the books to life, and which can also make certain elements of the story clearer that were perhaps difficult to understand on the page. Here are some popular and famous examples, but a little bit of research by your child can not only bring to light other links, but also improve their study skills.

Winnie-the-Pooh
Ashdown Forest, East Sussex

A. A. Milne used to live near the edge of the forest (which is actually more heathland than dense woodland) and frequently went for walks there. He based several of the locations in his imaginary Hundred Acre Wood on recognisable spots, as did the illustrator E. H. Shepard. So the Hundred Acre Wood itself is actually Five Hundred Acre Wood in real life, and 'Galleon's Leap' at the emotional end of *The House at Pooh Corner* is Gill's Lap, commemorated with an on-site plaque. You can find Pooh-themed walks at the official Ashdown Forest website (ashdownforest.org) and at their forest centre. Naturally, there is a bridge where you can play poohsticks. The whole experience is remarkably non-commercial and extremely beautiful, placed in the High Weald Area of Outstanding Natural Beauty.

The Weirdstone of Brisingamen
Alderley Edge, Cheshire

Alan Garner has spent his life around the Alderley Edge area, as did previous generations of his family, and his cult books *The Weirdstone of Brisingamen* and its sequel *The Moon of Gomrath* are set around real-life locations there, so you can actually follow the adventures of Susan and Colin on a map. You can visit the Wizard's Well and see its inscription 'Drink of this and take thy fill for the water falls by the Wizhard's will', reputedly carved by an ancestor of Garner's, as well as the (fake) Druid's Circle. Much of the countryside here is owned by the National Trust (nationaltrust.org.uk), who offer various walking suggestions around key locations. Garner also wrote about Alderley Edge in his *The Stone Book Quartet*, suitable for older children, while the village of Mow Cop and its folly right on the Cheshire–Staffordshire border play a central part in his book *Red Shift*.

Swallows and Amazons
Lake District and East Anglia

Arthur Ransome's *Swallows and Amazons* series has two main settings. The most famous for the books, later turned into films, is the Lake District. Although he was very familiar with the area, Ransome tended to amalgamate real-life spots for his locations: Wild Cat Island, where the children camp, is a mix of Peel Island in Coniston Water and Blake Holme in Windermere (in general the lake is like Windermere and the land around it like Coniston). Peel Island is owned by the National

Trust and you can take a ride on its steam yacht *Gondola* if you'd like a closer look. The fictional town of Rio is based on Bowness-on-Windermere.

While living in Suffolk, Ransome wrote *We Didn't Mean To Go To Sea* and *Secret Water*, both of which feature the hamlet of Pin Mill on the rural Shotley Peninsula, where Ransome had his own boats built.

You can still see Alma Cottage and the Butt and Oyster pub, which appear in the books. Ransome

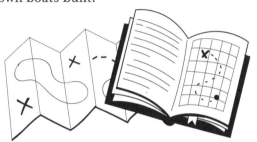

took fewer geographic liberties here than with his Lake District settings and mostly gave places their real names in these books. You can download a good walking trail of the Shotley area from the website of the Nancy Blackett Trust (nancyblackett.org). The village of Horning in Norfolk is central to two of Ransome's other children's adventure stories, *Coot Club* and *The Big Six*.

Watership Down
Ecchinswell, Hampshire

Many people are surprised to discover that the setting for *Watership Down* actually exists, as do many of the locations in Richard Adams's novel about rabbits, such as Nuthanger Farm and Honeycomb. Indeed, Adams even mentions the Ordnance Survey map reference (sheet 174) in the introduction. Reached via the village of Kingsclere, it is in fact part of the popular Wayfarer's Walk footpath.

The Children of Green Knowe
The Manor, Hemingford Grey, Cambridgeshire

The old house in Lucy M. Boston's series of Green Knowe stories is based, in quite some detail, on the author's home at the time of writing, in Cambridgeshire. So are her son Peter's illustrations for the books, including those of toys such as Tolly's carved mouse and the patched quilts mentioned in the stories, as well as the moated house and gardens themselves. Run by Lucy's daughter-in-law, Diana Boston, the garden is open daily but you need to book an appointment to visit the house except during May (greenknowe.co.uk).

Roald Dahl
Great Missenden, Buckinghamshire

The creator of *Charlie and the Chocolate Factory* lived in the village of Great Missenden for the last three decades of his life. His home, Gipsy House, is not open to the public (although it has previously been part of the National Garden Scheme so it is worth keeping an eye out in case it is again). However, other key locations are still to be seen, including the petrol pumps that inspired the garage in *Danny, the Champion of the World*, and the 'norphanage' from *The BFG*. Slightly further afield is Angling Spring Woods, which were the basis for the woods in *Danny*. Celebrating his life and work is the Roald Dahl Museum and Story Centre (roalddahl.com/museum), where you can find out much more about him, sit in his writing shed and take part in the regularly changing activities. You can also download two walking trails from the website which show you where to find key locations.

Harry Potter
Alnwick Castle, Northumberland (and many others)

While the locations for J. K. Rowling's hugely successful books are hard to pin down (Gandy Street in Exeter and the Shambles in York are both said to be inspirations for Diagon Alley), it's much easier when it comes to the films. *Harry Potter and the Philosopher's Stone* and *Harry Potter and the Chamber of Secrets* were both partly filmed at Alnwick Castle: Harry learns to fly his broomstick in the Outer Bailey and crashes the Weasleys' car in the Inner Bailey. Alnwick is also worth visiting for the excellent second-hand bookshop Barter Books.

When it comes to the films, there is a huge range of potential visits: the Great Hall at Hogwarts was modelled on the Great Hall at Christ Church in Oxford, while Leadenhall Market in London stood in for Diagon Alley and the Leaky Cauldron's facade. Visit Britain, the official tourist board of Great Britain, has plenty of information about filming locations at visitbritain.com. Also well worth a visit is Warner Bros. Studio Tour London: The Making of Harry Potter, near Watford, which offers a behind-the-scenes look at the making of the films. King's Cross railway station in central London also features in the books and films, and now has a dedicated Platform 9¾ photo opportunity, complete with a Hogwarts trolley half-disappearing into the wall.

The Secret Garden
Great Maytham Hall, near Tenterden, Kent

The gardens at Great Maytham Hall inspired Frances Hodgson Burnett to write *The Secret Garden*. While living there at the turn of the twentieth century, she discovered an abandoned walled garden dating back to the early eighteenth century, and restored it herself, writing in the garden's gazebo surrounded by the roses she planted. The Hall is now private apartments, but the gardens, rebuilt by Sir Edwin Lutyens, can be visited on certain dates in the spring and summer as part of the National Garden Scheme (ngs.org.uk).

There are many more places with links to authors and their works, and organisations like the National Trust (nationaltrust.org.uk) and English Heritage (www. english-heritage.org.uk) not only own important sites but also run frequent literary activities. Children who enjoy Beatrix Potter's animal stories will also like her home at Hill Top Farm in the Lake District. Similarly, older children who have read Rosemary Sutcliff's *The Eagle of the Ninth* about the disappearance of a Roman legion will get a lot out of a visit to Hadrian's Wall: Housesteads Roman Fort in Northumberland is particularly atmospheric.

And don't forget that many of these properties also have strong non-fiction connections, such as Charles Darwin's home at Down House in Kent, where he wrote *On the Origin of Species*, or Isaac Newton's at Woolsthorpe Manor in Lincolnshire, where his apple tree is (allegedly) still going strong. Both have excellent interactive exhibitions. For those interested in the history of the Second World War and codebreaking, a trip to Bletchley Park near Milton Keynes is a must.

Useful books to start your research include *Adventure Walks for Families in and around London* (with a much wider geographic spread than the title implies) by Becky Jones and Clare Lewis, and *Where was Wonderland?: A Traveller's Guide to the Settings of Classic Children's Books* by Frank

Barrett. Older children may also enjoy *Literary Places*, written by Sarah Baxter and illustrated by Amy Grimes.

BOOK TOWNS

Visiting bookshops with children is a real pleasure and the UK is among the many countries in the world that have several rural book towns, full of mainly second-hand bookshops and book-related industries. The movement was started by Richard Booth in Hay-on-Wye in Wales in the 1960s. As well as the huge annual festival, there are many booksellers in the town including the enormous Richard Booth's Bookshop, which is also home to a forty-seven-seat cinema and cafe. Elsewhere in the town there is the Hay Cinema Bookshop, a former picturehouse that claims to have the world's largest open-air bookshop, and the Children's Bookshop, just outside the town, selling only children's titles with an emphasis on twentieth-century fiction. Also good for children's and illustrated books is Rose's Books.

Scotland's book town is Wigtown in Dumfries and Galloway. Like Hay, it also runs an excellent annual literary festival as well as a special one – Big DoG – focusing entirely on children's books. Wigtown is home to Scotland's largest second-hand bookshop, The Bookshop, and among the various publishers in town is the small independent Curly Tale Books, run from the former Box of Frogs children's bookshop, and which continues to sell titles for younger readers. More details at wigtown-booktown.co.uk.

England has its own book town in Sedbergh near Kendal, within the Yorkshire Dales National Park. The largest bookshop is the huge Westwood Books, though, unusually for a book town, several of its booksellers are not entirely dedicated to books – but still find space for a book section! Visit sedberghbooktown.co.uk for more information on what titles the local fish and chip shop stocks.

BOOK-BASED ATTRACTIONS

In addition to locations, there are numerous dedicated book-themed attractions. Seven Stories – the National Centre for Children's Books in Newcastle upon Tyne – is focused on a huge range of children's literary history over seven floors, styling itself as 'the first and only museum in the UK wholly dedicated to the art of British children's books'. As well as spaces to encourage children to write and draw, it also holds an enormous archive of original manuscripts and illustrations, from the 1930s to the present day, a highlight of which is the early drafts of *The Giant Alexander* created by Frank Herrmann and George Him; unpublished playscripts by Philip Pullman can be seen on its website at sevenstories.org.uk. They use this material to present exhibitions featuring characters such as David McKee's Elmer the Patchwork Elephant. Seven Stories also runs short courses for parents about how to encourage children to read.

Discover Children's Story Centre (discover.org.uk) is in Stratford, London, and is aimed at families with children up to to eleven years old. Their creative play spaces inspire children to make up stories and their changing interactive exhibitions focus on popular children's authors. The centre runs workshops with authors and illustrators all through the year, and has a well-stocked children's bookshop.

The Story Museum in Oxford is currently undergoing a major redevelopment to its exhibitions and galleries. It plans to reopen in the spring of 2020 with a Treasure Chamber, Enchanted Library, Small Worlds early years gallery, The Shed theatre space and the City of Stories digital experience, introducing the literary history of Oxford. In the meantime it has been continuing its outreach work as well as holding some events on site. Check its website at storymuseum.org.uk for updates.

Though not specifically aimed at children, other author venues often also run children's activities so it's worth keeping an eye out for possibilities. The Johnson Birthplace Museum in Lichfield, for example, runs regular Words Alive events on Saturday mornings for children to enjoy some reading, writing and acting (samueljohnsonbirthplace.org.uk). Similarly, the House of Illustration art gallery in London often runs illustration activities for children and puts on exhibitions featuring the work of children's book illustrators such as the creator of the Madeline books, Ludwig Bemelmans. In 2019 it opened its From the Studio permanent space, an evolving exhibit containing current work by the illustrator Quentin Blake (houseofillustration.org.uk). The Centre for Literacy in Primary Education (CLPE) also has a wonderfully curated Literacy Library of 23,000 children's titles which parents can visit for inspiration about what to read next (clpe.org.uk/clpe/library).

BOOK FESTIVALS

Authors and illustrators regularly appear at signing events or give talks at bookshops, but one of the best ways to catch your children's favourite writers (and discover new ones) is at a book festival. In 2012, my children had only just started reading Cressida Cowell's *How to Train Your Dragon* books, but after seeing her speak at the first Hoo's Kids Book Fest at Luton Hoo that year, they were hugely motivated to read more in the series.

Barnes Children's Literature Festival

Organisers claim this is London's largest dedicated children's literature festival. As well as the annual weekend events, there is a special outreach element to state primary schools in the capital (barneskidslitfest.org).

Bath Children's Literature Festival

A huge gathering over the space of a fortnight makes this the largest literature festival for children in Europe (bathfestivals.org.uk/childrens-literature).

Imagine Children's Festival

Held at London's Southbank Centre, this is a twelve-day celebration of the written word in theatre and literature. A large proportion of the events are free (southbankcentre.co.uk).

Northern Children's Book Festival

This is not based at a single location; rather, organisers run two weeks of events across the north-east of England, working especially closely with schools and libraries (northernchildrensbookfestival.org.uk).

Shrewsbury Bookfest

The first children's literary festival, this was established in 1999 and is run on a not-for-profit basis, largely by volunteers, on the first May Bank Holiday weekend (shrewsburybookfest.co.uk).

As well as festivals aimed solely at children, most of the bigger literary festivals also run extensive children's programmes. HAYDAYS is the Hay Festival's children's section (hayfestival.com/wales/haydays) with events, workshops and demonstrations aimed at all ages, including the Hay Festival Compass which focuses on older teenagers. The Baillie Gifford Children's Programme is part of the Edinburgh International Book Festival and includes more than 200 events for younger readers. Both attract a genuinely international range of writers and illustrators. Also worth looking out for is YALC, the Young Adult Literature Convention, which is held annually as part of the London Film and Comic Con in London. The former Children's Laureate Malorie Blackman was one of the guiding forces in establishing YALC in 2014, and it has become a popular event for readers of YA.

Indeed, there are plenty of comics conventions around the country. MCM Comic Con (mcmcomiccon.com) run events in Birmingham, Manchester, Glasgow and London that cover a huge range of manga, comic books, film and sci-fi. Also worth looking at is Lew Stringer's blog. Lew has been a comics artist for decades, with a long list of titles under his belt, such as *Buster*, *Dandy* and *Beano*. He attends comic conventions around the

UK and conveniently provides links and dates on his site (lewstringercomics.blogspot.co.uk).

Other festivals with children's sections to look out for include the Cheltenham Literature Festival (cheltenham festivals.com), the Henley Literary Festival (henley literaryfestival.co.uk), the Oxford Literary Festival (oxfordliteraryfestival.org) and the Essex Book Festival (essexbookfestival.org.uk). There are many more around the UK so look out for your local ones: literaryfestivals. co.uk is quite an encyclopedic resource.

If your child is also interested in music and songwriting, you might consider going to one of the many folk festivals around the country. Performers such as Grace Petrie and Billy Bragg, whose lyrics are at least as important as their music, are exciting acts to watch live. Folk by the Oak at Hatfield House in Hertfordshire is a good starting point as it is only one day long, held every July (folkbytheoak.com).

The public library service is a national treasure. Libraries are treasure houses for the mind. Physically, they provide a safe space for everyone and anyone to come in, without obligation, to sit, explore, discover, investigate, enjoy and research. Where there are cafes and spaces away from the study areas, they are also places where we can meet and talk. Where libraries have societies, meetings and events, we find ourselves in larger groups from across our locality.

So libraries are not and never have been simply a place where you borrow a book – great though that is in itself. They are places where we can extend ourselves beyond who we are. I mean that in two ways: we extend ourselves in terms of finding out things or reading things that we haven't read or seen before; we extend ourselves in terms of finding ourselves with other people in this public space.

Why or how any of this should ever be starved of funds, why or how any of this should have been curtailed through closures is to my mind criminal. This has been a restriction on our rights as citizens. The duty of government is of course to protect us but also to nurture its citizens to enable us as individuals and as a society to progress and grow.

Though the service is universal, there are groups for whom it is especially important: children from homes without books, recent migrants, the poor, people in need of advice and information and who don't have the knowledge or the means to get access to information in any other way, young people studying where the home environment is not suitable or ideal.

I have no problem with ideas for making libraries multi-purpose, combining them with other services, so long as the core offer is to do with knowledge, imagination and information. I have a strong sense that this is because the core focus is on language. I also believe that for libraries to be attractive and useful we need trained, experienced, committed and well-paid people – librarians! – to be at the heart of the service. For people to be able to access what libraries offer, we need people to take us to whatever is the next step, the human bridge between where we are and where we might be.

Michael Rosen is a poet, writer and broadcaster. He was Children's Laureate 2007–2009 and is Professor of Children's Literature at Goldsmiths, University of London.

Like many other parents, I despair at my children. Take Henry, who is fourteen. His only interest appears to be *Fortnite*, the evil addictive product of a group of uber geeks. These geeks happily make millions out of destroying families. Henry will happily spend five hours playing *Fortnite* with his mates. But when I ask him to practise his guitar, he makes an enormous fuss. He finally trudges up to his room, plays it for ten minutes and then sneaks back down to the computer. He also appears addicted to an American ad sales scam called YouTube.

Luckily he does read George R. R. Martin books, which is something, and is therefore capable of concentrating. When the children were small, we had no TV, which I think helped. They certainly did not have phones or computer games. So they did at least read books when they were little. But the gadgets started to creep in when the eldest was around eleven, and it has been impossible to prevent their invasion since then.

One answer would be to do nothing at all about this problem, and simply set a good example by reading lots of books yourself, in obvious places around the house. This way you would set a good example, and if they don't follow, that's their tough luck. I would also recommend taking them on holiday to Landmark Trust houses, places where there is no Wi-Fi or TV. Screens now compete with books, but remember that in Jane Austen's day young people were told off for reading too many novels and writing too many letters. So we should probably worry less.

Tom Hodgkinson, editor of the Idler *magazine*

Helpful sources

Magazines

Beano Beano.com

Doctor Who Magazine doctorwhomagazine.com

First News firstnews.co.uk

Phoenix thephoenixcomic.co.uk

Scoop scoopthemag.co.uk

Sonshine sonshinemagazine.com – issue 4 is all about books

The Week Junior theweekjunior.co.uk

Organisations

Bodleian Libraries www.bodleian.ox.ac.uk

Book Trust booktrust.org.uk

British Library bl.uk

Centre for Literacy in Primary Education clpe.org.uk

Children's Poetry Archive childrens.poetryarchive.org

English Heritage www.english-heritage.org.uk

Federation of Children's Book Groups fcbg.org.uk

Listening Books listening-books.org.uk

National Garden Scheme ngs.org.uk

National Literacy Trust literacytrust.org.uk

National Poetry Library nationalpoetrylibrary.org.uk

National Trust nationaltrust.org.uk

Poetry Book Society poetrybooks.co.uk

Poetry Society poetrysociety.org.uk

Reading Agency readingagency.org.uk

Scottish Book Trust scottishbooktrust.com

Book Attractions

Discover Children's Story Centre discover.org.uk

House of Illustration houseofillustration.org.uk

Roald Dahl Museum and Story Centre roalddahl.com

Seven Stories – The National Centre for Children's Books
    sevenstories.org.uk

Story Museum storymuseum.org.uk

Websites

Books for Keeps booksforkeeps.co.uk

CLPE Corebooks website clpe.org.uk/corebooks

CLPE Poetryline website clpe.org.uk/poetryline

CLPE **Power of Pictures website** clpe.org.uk/
    powerofpictures
Goodreads goodreads.com
HarperCollins epicreads.com
Letterbox Library letterboxlibrary.com
LibraryThing librarything.com
Mantra Lingua www.mantralingua.com
Pen and Inc cilip.org.uk/general/custom.
    asp?page=penandinc
Penguin penguinteen.com
Penguin Random House readbrightly.com
Walker Books picturebookparty.co.uk

Useful Further Reading

Help your Child Love Reading by Alison David
*Deconstructing Penguins: Parents, Kids, and the Bond of
    Reading* by Lawrence and Nancy Goldstone
*The Enchanted Hour: The Miraculous Power of Reading Aloud in
    the Age of Distraction* by Meghan Cox Gurdon
The Pleasures of Reading in an Age of Distraction by Alan Jacobs
The Read-Aloud Family by Sarah Mackenzie
Bookworm: A Memoir of Childhood Reading by Lucy Mangan
The Reading Promise: My Father and the Books We Shared by
    Alice Ozma
*My Life with Bob: Flawed Heroine Keeps Book of Books, Plot
    Ensues* by Pamela Paul

How to Raise a Reader by Pamela Paul and Maria Russo

Good Ideas: How to Be your Child's Best Teacher by Michael Rosen

Why Write? Why Read? by Michael Rosen

Why You Should Read Children's Books, Even Though You Are So Old and Wise by Katherine Rundell

On Rereading by Patricia Meyer Spacks

The Child that Books Built by Francis Spufford

Raising Kids Who Read by Daniel T. Willingham

Helping your Child to Read by Annemarie Young

CHILDREN'S BOOKS MENTIONED

(for age-specific suggestions, see reading recommendations from the CLPE, pp. 181–204)

Introduction

Buzzy Bear Goes Camping by Dorothy Marino

The Boy at the Back of the Class by Onjali Q. Raúf

Nutshell Library by Maurice Sendak

Chapter One

Asterix books written by René Goscinny, illustrated by Albert Uderzo (the entire collection, even the later ones)

Tintin books by Hergé (the entire collection, with exceptions)

Jennings series by Anthony Buckeridge (especially the
    earlier ones)
Still William by Richmal Crompton
The works of Alan Garner (especially the *Stone Book Quartet*)
The Hate U Give by Angie Thomas
The Wolves of Willoughby Chase by Joan Aiken
Ladybird books

Chapter Two

Mr Men and *Little Miss* books by Adam and Roger
    Hargreaves
The Borrowers by Mary Norton
Beowulf (various versions including those by Kevin
    Crossley-Holland and Michael Morpurgo)
The Lorax by Dr Seuss
The Wind in the Willows by Kenneth Grahame
Samuel Pepys's diary
The works of Richard Scarry
Blown Away by Rob Biddulph
The Hobbit and *The Lord of the Rings* series by J. R. R. Tolkien
The Elephant and the Bad Baby by Elfrida Vipont, illustrated
    by Raymond Briggs
Tim Mouse by Judy Brook
Mr Rabbit and the Lovely Present by Charlotte Zolotow,
    illustrated by Maurice Sendak

The Gruffalo by Julia Donaldson

Each Peach Pear Plum by Allan Ahlberg

Shark in the Park by Nick Sharratt

Going Shopping by Sarah Garland

The Princess Bride by William Goldman

Treasure Island by Robert Louis Stevenson

The Three Musketeers by Alexandre Dumas (various child-friendly versions are available)

English Fairy Tales and Legends by Rosalind Kerven

The Restless Girls by Jessie Burton

Pretty Salma by Niki Daly

Little People, Big Dreams series, created by Maria Isabel Sánchez Vegara

The Witches by Roald Dahl

The Hundred and One Dalmatians by Dodie Smith

Harry Potter series by J. K. Rowling

Mister Magnolia by Quentin Blake

The Surprise Party by Pat Hutchins

The Father Christmas Joke Book by Raymond Briggs

Andy Pandy's in the Country by Maria Bird

Katie Morag Delivers the Mail by Mairi Hedderwick

Happy Christmas Maisy by Lucy Cousins

Little Red Train books by Benedict Blathwayt

Noggin the Nog series (especially *The Omruds*) by Oliver Postgate and Peter Firmin

Railway series books by Rev. W. Awdry

A Child's Christmas in Wales by Dylan Thomas, illustrated by Edward Ardizzone

The Secret Path (one of the Percy the Park Keeper series) by Nick Butterworth

A Rabbit in the Attic by Jane Brett, illustrated by Francine Oomen

The Lost Words by Robert Macfarlane, illustrated by Jackie Morris

Maps by Aleksandra and Daniel Mizieliński

A Street through Time by Anne Millard, illustrated by Steve Noon

The Midnight Folk and *The Box of Delights* by John Masefield

A Bear Called Paddington by Michael Bond

The Wonderful Wizard of Oz and *The Tin Woodman of Oz* by L. Frank Baum

The works of Judy Blume

The Sword in the Stone by T. H. White

Just William by Richmal Crompton

CHERUB series by Robert Muchamore

Alfred Hitchcock and the Three Investigators by William Arden

Accidental series by Tom McLaughlin (especially *The Accidental Prime Minister*)

Wild trilogy by Piers Torday (*The Last Wild, Dark Wild, The Wild Beyond*)

Track series by Jason Reynolds (*Ghost, Patina, Sunny, Lu*)

The Lion, the Witch and the Wardrobe by C. S. Lewis

Black Beauty by Anna Sewell

Percy Jackson series by Rick Riordan

How to Train Your Dragon series and *Wizards of Once* series
    by Cressida Cowell

The Tiger who Came to Tea by Judith Kerr

Just So Stories by Rudyard Kipling

Chapter Three

I Can Read With My Eyes Shut! by Dr Seuss

The Diary of Anne Frank by Anne Frank

The Journey by Francesca Sanna

Where Children Sleep and *Playground* by James Mollison

Horrible Histories by Terry Deary

Hidden Figures by Margot Lee Shetterly

How to Make a Human Out of Soup by Tracey Turner,
    illustrated by Sally Kindberg

Tiny by Nicola Davies, illustrated by Emily Sutton

Shackleton's Journey by William Grill

Katie and the Spanish Princess by James Mayhew

As I Walked Out One Midsummer Morning by Laurie Lee

Private Peaceful by Michael Morpurgo

A Wrinkle In Time by Madeleine L'Engle

Alastair Humphreys' Great Adventurers by Alastair
    Humphreys, illustrated by Kevin Ward

Tunneling to Freedom by Nel Yomtov, illustrated by
    Alessandro Valdrighi

The 14th Dalai Lama by Tetsu Saiwai

Sally Heathcote, Suffragette by Mary and Bryan Talbot,
  illustrated by Kate Charlesworth

Anne Frank's Diary by Ari Folman

Suffragette: The Battle for Equality by David Roberts

The Rattle Bag, edited by Seamus Heaney and Ted Hughes

Read Me and Laugh: A Funny Poem for Every Day of the Year,
  edited by Gaby Morgan

Four Feet and Two, compiled by Leila Berg

England: Poems from a School, edited by Kate Clanchy

Chapter four

The Little Prince by Antoine de Saint-Exupéry

Bibliophile series by Jane Mount

Frankie's Magic Football by Frank Lampard

T. J. series by Theo Walcott

Evie's Magic Bracelet by Jessica Ennis-Hill

Magic Ballerina books by Darcey Bussell

Flying Fergus by Chris Hoy

Kid Normal books by Greg James and Chris Smith

The Falcon Chronicles by Steve Backshall

Odd and the Frost Giants and *Norse Mythology* by Neil Gaiman

The Sleeping Army by Francesca Simon

We See Everything by William Sutcliffe

*The Thrilling Adventures of Lovelace and Babbage: The (Mostly)
  True Story of the First Computer* by Sydney Padua

Sisters and Champions: The True Story of Venus and Serena Williams by Howard Bryant

Splash by Charli Howard

Before John was a Jazz Giant: A Song of John Coltrane by Carole Boston Weatherford, illustrated by Sean Qualls

My Museum by Joanne Liu

Kid Artists: True Tales of Childhood from Creative Legends by David Stabler, illustrated by Doogie Horner

Frida Kahlo and her Animalitos by Monica Brow, illustrated by John Parra

The Wizard's Cookbook by Aurélia Beaupommier

Moomins Cookbook: An Introduction to Finnish Cookery by Tove Jansson and Sami Malila

The Secret Garden Cookbook by Amy Cotler

The Little Library Cookbook by Kate Young

Bake Me a Story by Nadiya Hussain

Famous Five books by Enid Blyton

Five Go Feasting: Famously Good Recipes by Josh Sutton

Jolly Good Food by Allegra McEvedy

My Family and Other Animals by Gerald Durrell

Dining with the Durrells by David Shimwell

Chapter five

His Dark Materials trilogy by Philip Pullman

The Children of Green Knowe by Lucy M. Boston

Wimpy Kid series by Jeff Kinney

The World of Norm series by Jonathan Meres

Illegal by Eoin Colfer and Andrew Donkin, illustrated by
    Giovanni Rigano

Dark Satanic Mills by Marcus and Julian Sedgwick

The Marvels and *The Invention of Hugo Cabret* by Brian
    Selznick

Tom's Midnight Garden by Philippa Pearce

Artemis Fowl series by Eoin Colfer

American Born Chinese by Gene Luen Yang

Atticus the Storyteller by Lucy Coates

Stig of the Dump by Clive King

The works of Roald Dahl, Cressida Cowell and
    David Walliams

Wolf Brother by Michelle Paver

Skulduggery Pleasant series by Derek Landy

A Song of Ice and Fire by George R. R. Martin

Chapter Six

Littlenose stories by John Grant

Winnie-the-Pooh and *The House at Pooh Corner* by A. A. Milne

Swallows and Amazons series and other works by Arthur
    Ransome

Watership Down by Richard Adams

The Secret Garden by Frances Hodgson Burnett

The works of Beatrix Potter

The Eagle of the Ninth by Rosemary Sutcliff

Adventure Walks for Families in and around London by Becky
Jones and Clare Lewis

*Where was Wonderland?: A Traveller's Guide to the Settings of
Classic Children's Books* by Frank Barrett

Literary Places by Sarah Baxter, illustrated by Amy Grimes

The Giant Alexander by Frank Herrmann and George Him

Reading recommendations from the CLPE

(Centre for Literacy in Primary Education)

STARTING TO READ
Ages 3-5

Encouraging reading

Big Box, Little Box by Caryl Hart, illustrated by Edward Underwood

So Much by Trish Cooke, illustrated by Helen Oxenbury

We're Going on a Bear Hunt by Michael Rosen, illustrated by Helen Oxenbury

When's My Birthday? by Julie Fogliano, illustrated by Christian Robinson

Mister Magnolia by Quentin Blake

Orange, Pear, Apple, Bear by Emily Gravett

Colin and Lee, Carrot and Pea by Morag Hood

A Royal Lullabyhullaballoo! by Mick Inkpen

Please, Mr Panda by Steve Antony

Quiet! by Kate Alizadeh

Developing reading

Alfie Gets in First by Shirley Hughes

Knuffle Bunny by Mo Willems

Ruby's Sword by Jaqueline Véissid, illustrated by Paola
    Zakimi

Lulu Loves the Library by Anna McQuinn, illustrated by
    Rosalind Beardshaw

Can't You Sleep, Little Bear? by Martin Waddell, illustrated by
    Barbara Firth

Stanley's Stick by John Hegley, illustrated by Neal Layton

No Dinner! by Jessica Souhami

Bedtime for Monsters by Ed Vere

Naughty Bus by Jan and Jerry Oke

Lost and Found by Oliver Jeffers

Ages 5-7

Encouraging reading

Hairy Maclary from Donaldson's Dairy by Lynley Dodd

Billy and the Beast by Nadia Shireen

Wolf Won't Bite! by Emily Gravett

Would You Rather? by John Burningham

Daisy: Eat Your Peas by Kes Gray, illustrated by Nick Sharratt

Little Rabbit Foo Foo by Michael Rosen, illustrated by Arthur Robins

Mr Scruff by Simon James

Dare! by Lorna Gutierrez, illustrated by Polly Noakes

This Book Just Ate My Dog! by Richard Byrne

Where the Wild Things Are by Maurice Sendak

Developing reading

Anna Hibiscus series by Atinuke and Lauren Tobia

That Rabbit Belongs to Emily Brown by Cressida Cowell, illustrated by Neal Layton

Winnie-the-Pooh by A. A. Milne, illustrated by E. H. Shepard

Kevin by Rob Biddulph

Look Up! by Nathan Bryon, illustrated by Dapo Adeola

Rapunzel / Little Red / Hansel and Gretel by Bethan Woollvin

Rabbit and Bear series by Julian Gough, illustrated by Jim Field

The Snail and the Whale by Julia Donaldson, illustrated by Axel Scheffler

Farmer Duck by Martin Waddell, illustrated by Helen Oxenbury

The Jolly Postman or Other People's Letters by Janet and Allan Ahlberg

Ages 7-9

Encouraging reading

Angry Arthur by Hiawyn Oram, illustrated by Satoshi Kitamura

Grandpa Green by Lane Smith

Me and You by Anthony Browne

Dinosaurs and All That Rubbish by Michael Foreman

The Wall in the Middle of the Book by Jon Agee

Wolves by Emily Gravett

Chicken, Clicking by Jeanne Willis, illustrated by Tony Ross

Good Little Wolf by Nadia Shireen

Horrid Henry series by Francesca Simon, illustrated by Tony Ross

Car Wash Wish by Sita Brahmachari

Developing reading

Moon Man by Tomi Ungerer

The Wild Robot / The Wild Robot Escapes by Peter Brown

Varjak Paw / The Outlaw Varjak Paw by S. F. Said, illustrated by Dave McKean

Oliver and the Seawigs / Cakes in Space / Pugs of the Frozen North / Jinks and O'Hare, Funfair Repair by Philip Reeve and Sarah McIntyre

Pippi Longstocking by Astrid Lindgren, illustrated by Lauren Child

The Boy at the Back of the Class by Onjali Q. Raúf

The Accidental Prime Minister / Secret Agent / Billionaire / Father Christmas / President / Rock Star by Tom McLaughlin

Libba: The Magnificent Musical Life of Elizabeth Cotton by Laura Veirs, illustrated by Tatyana Fazlalizadeh

The Imaginary by A. F. Harrold, illustrated by Emily Gravett

The Iron Man by Ted Hughes, illustrated by Laura Carlin

Ages 9–11

Encouraging reading

Corey's Rock by Sita Brahmachari, illustrated by Jane Ray

Life Doesn't Frighten Me by Maya Angelou, illustrated by Jean-Michel Basquiat

Red and the City by Marie Voigt

Wolves in the Walls / The Day I Swapped My Dad for Two Goldfish by Neil Gaiman, illustrated by Dave McKean

The Promise by Nicola Davies, illustrated by Laura Carlin

You're a Bad Man, Mr Gum! by Andy Stanton, illustrated by David Tazzyman

War and Peas by Michael Foreman

The Blurred Man and I Know What You Did Last Wednesday by Anthony Horowitz

A Story Like the Wind by Gill Lewis, illustrated by Jo Weaver

A Boy and a Bear in a Boat by Dave Shelton

Developing reading

Beetle Boy / *Beetle Queen* / *Battle of the Beetles* by M. G. Leonard

Cosmic by Frank Cottrell-Boyce

Harry Miller's Run by David Almond, illustrated by Salvatore Rubbino

Mortal Engines by Philip Reeve

Pax by Sara Pennypacker, illustrated by Jon Klassen

Pig Heart Boy by Malorie Blackman

Running on Empty by S. E. Durrant

The Last Wild / *The Dark Wild* / *The Wild Beyond* by Piers Torday

Phoenix by S. F. Said, illustrated by Dave McKean

Where the River Runs Gold by Sita Brahmachari

HOW TO GO PLACES: THE IMPORTANCE OF NON-FICTION
Ages 3-5

Information texts

Yucky Worms by Vivian French and Jessica Ahlberg

Counting with Tiny Cat by Viviane Schwarz

Once Upon a Star by James Carter, illustrated by Mar Hernández

Our Very Own Dog / *Our Very Own Cat* by Amanda McCardie, illustrated by Salvatore Rubbino

Beware of the Crocodile by Martin Jenkins, illustrated by Satoshi Kitamura

Blackbird, Blackbird, What Do You Do? by Kate McLelland

Dig, Dig, Digging / Emergency! by Margaret Mayo, illustrated by Alex Ayliffe

Because of an Acorn by Lola M. and Alex Schaefer, illustrated by Frann Preston-Gannon

Rain by Manya Stojic

Astro Girl by Ken Wilson-Max

Poetry

A Great Big Cuddle by Michael Rosen, illustrated by Chris Riddell

Out and About by Shirley Hughes

Stomp, Chomp, Big Roars! Here Come the Dinosaurs by Kaye Umansky, illustrated by Nick Sharratt

Zim, Zam, Zoom! by James Carter, illustrated by Nicola Colton

Here We Go Round the Mulberry Bush illustrated by Sophie Fatus

I Wish I Had a Pirate Hat by Roger Stevens, illustrated by Lorna Scobie

Here's a Little Poem edited by Jane Yolen and Andrew Fusek Peters, illustrated by Polly Dunbar

I See the Moon: Poems and Rhymes for Bedtime by Rosalind Beardshaw

Read to your Baby Every Day edited by Rachel Williams, embroidered by Chloe Giordano

The Oxford Treasury of Nursery Rhymes illustrated by Ian Beck

READING RECOMMENDATIONS

Ages 5-7

Information texts

A First Book of Nature by Nicola Davies, illustrated by Mark
Hearld

Caterpillar, Butterfly by Vivian French, illustrated by
Charlotte Voake

It Starts With a Seed by Laura Knowles, illustrated by Jennie
Webber

Professor Astro Cat's Solar System by Dominic Walliman,
illustrated by Ben Newman

*The Big Book of Bugs / The Big Book of the Blue / The Big Book
of Birds / The Big Book of Beasts* by Yuval Zommer

Shadow by Robie H. Harris, illustrated by Patrick Benson

The Great Big Book of Families by Mary Hoffman, illustrated
by Ros Asquith

Lifesize / Lifesize Dinosaurs by Sophy Henn

All Kinds of Cars by Carl Johanson

What's Under the Bed? A book about the Earth beneath us by
Mick Manning, illustrated by Brita Granström

Poetry

The Puffin Book of Fantastic First Poems edited by June Crebbin

Thinker: My Puppy Poet and Me by Eloise Greenfield,
illustrated by Ehsan Abdollahi

How to be a Tiger by George Szirtes, illustrated by Tim
Archbold

I Am the Seed That Grew the Tree edited by Fiona Waters,
  illustrated by Frann Preston-Gannon

Tasty Poems by Jill Bennett, illustrated by Nick Sharratt

Heard it in the Playground by Allan Ahlberg, illustrated by
  Fritz Wegner

Poems to Perform by Julia Donaldson, illustrated by Clare
  Melinsky

My Village: Rhymes from Around the World edited by Danielle
  Wright, illustrated by Mique Moriuchi

Even My Ears Are Smiling by Michael Rosen, illustrated by
  Babette Cole

Little Miss Muffet and Other Rhymes by Patrick George

Ages 7-9

Information texts

Wild Animals of the North by Dieter Braun

Poo! A Natural History of the Unmentionable by Nicola Davies,
  illustrated by Neal Layton

Africa, Amazing Africa by Atinuke, illustrated by Mouni Feddag

Curiosity: The Story of a Mars Rover by Markus Motum

Atlas of Adventures by Rachel Williams, illustrated by Lucy
  Letherland

Can We Save the Tiger? by Martin Jenkins, illustrated by
  Vicky White

Mami Miti: Wangari Maathai and the Trees of Kenya by Donna
  Jo Napoli, illustrated by Kadir Nelson

Rosa Parks by Lisbeth Kaiser, illustrated by Marta Antelo, one
of the *Little People, Big Dreams* series.

Welcome to the Museum series: *Dinosaurium* by Chris
Wormell and Lily Murray / *Historium* by Jo Nelson and
Richard Wilkinson / *Planetarium* by Raman Prinja and
Chris Wormell / *Botanicum* by Kathy Willis and Katie
Scott / *Anatomicum* by Jennifer Z. Paxton and Katy
Wiedemann / *Animalium* by Jenny Broom and Katie Scott
/ *The Story of Life* by Ruth Symons and Katie Scott

*Discover... The Roman Empire / The Ancient Egyptians / The
Ancient Aztecs / The Ancient Greeks* by Isabel and Imogen
Greenberg

Poetry

Jelly Boots, Smelly Boots by Michael Rosen, illustrated by
David Tazzyman

Werewolf Club Rules by Joseph Coelho, illustrated by John
O'Leary

All the Best by Roger McGough, illustrated by Lydia Monks

A Kid in My Class by Rachel Rooney, illustrated by Chris
Riddell

Things You Find in a Poet's Beard by A. F. Harrold, illustrated
by Chris Riddell

Moon Juice by Kate Wakeling, illustrated by Elīna Brasliņa

Where Zebras Go by Sue Hardy Dawson

Dancing in the Rain by John Lyons

Chicken on the Roof by Matt Goodfellow, illustrated by
    Hannah Asen

Lost Magic: The Very Best of Brian Moses illustrated by Ed Boxall

Ages 9-11

Information texts

A World of Information by James Brown and Richard Platt

Suffragette: The Battle for Equality by David Roberts

Anatomy: A Cutaway Look Inside the Human Body by Helene
    Druvert and Jean-Claude Druvert

The Earth Book by Jonathan Litton, illustrated by Thomas
    Hegbrook

Endangered Animals by Martin Jenkins, illustrated by Tom
    Frost

*What is Right and Wrong? Who Decides? Where do Values Come
    From? And Other Big Questions* by Michael Rosen and
    Annemarie Young

Timeline: A Visual History of Our World by Peter Goes

Freedom by Catherine Johnson

Coming to England by Floella Benjamin

Professor Astro Cat's Frontiers of Space by Dominic Walliman,
    illustrated by Ben Newman

Poetry

Michael Rosen's Big Book of Bad Things by Michael Rosen,
    illustrated by Joe Berger

The Rainmaker Danced by John Agard, illustrated by Satoshi
   Kitamura

Cosmic Disco by Grace Nichols, illustrated by Alice Wright

Booked by Kwame Alexander

*A Poem for Every Night of the Year / A Poem for Every Day of the
   Year* edited by Allie Esiri

Overheard in a Tower Block by Joseph Coelho, illustrated by
   Kate Milner

The Highwayman by Alfred Tennyson, illustrated by Charles
   Keeping

Dark Sky Park by Philip Gross, illustrated by Jesse Hodgson

Love that Dog by Sharon Creech

Rhythm and Poetry by Karl Nova

HOW TO ENCOURAGE THEIR READING
Ages 3-5

General

Where's Lenny? by Ken Wilson-Max

Lulu's First Day by Anna McQuinn, illustrated by Rosalind
   Beardshaw

The Hueys in None the Number by Oliver Jeffers

When I Grow Up... by Patrick George

Happy in Our Skin by Fran Manushkin, illustrated by Lauren
   Tobia

Errol's Garden by Gillian Hibbs

Roadwork / Construction / Demolition / Ambulance, Ambulance! by Sally Sutton, illustrated by Brian Lovelock

A First Book of Animals by Nicola Davies, illustrated by Petr Horáček

Hello, Mr Dinosaur / Hello Mrs Elephant by Sam Boughton

Trees by Carme Lemniscates

Cookery and food

Oliver's Vegetables / Oliver's Fruit Salad / Oliver's Milkshake by Vivian French and Alison Bartlett

Gruffalo Crumble and Other Recipes by Julia Donaldson and Axel Scheffler

I Can Cook! by Sally Brown and Kate Morris

Nadiya's Bake Me a Story by Nadiya Hussain, illustrated by Clair Rossiter

Ages 5–7

General

What Are You Playing At? by Marie-Sabine Roger, illustrated by Anne Sol

A Book of Feelings by Amanda McCardie, illustrated by Salvatore Rubbino

How Big is Big? How Far is Far? All Around Me illustrated by Jun Cen

My First Book of Birds illustrated by Zoë Ingram

Space Kids: An Introduction for Young Explorers by Andrea De Santis and Steve Parker

The Skies Above My Eyes / The Street Beneath My Feet by Charlotte Guillain, illustrated by Yuval Zommer

The Amazing Dinosaur Detectives by Maggie Li

Over and Under the Pond / Up in the Garden and Down in the Dirt by Kate Messner, illustrated by Christopher Silas Neal

How to Build a City by Isabel Otter, illustrated by Harry Woodgate

Winter Sleep: A Hibernation Story by Sean Taylor and Alex Morss, illustrated by Cinyee Chiu

Ages 7-9

General

How to Make Awesome Comics! by Neill Cameron

Tell Me a Picture by Quentin Blake

Odd Science: Amazing Inventions by James Olstein

A World of Your Own by Laura Carlin

Bones: An Inside Look at the Animal Kingdom by Jules Howard, illustrated by Chervelle Fryer

101 Things for Kids to Do Outside / 101 Brilliant Things for Kids to Do with Science by Dawn Isaac

Little Leaders: Visionary Women From Around the World by Vashti Harrison

Unseen Worlds, Real Life Microscopic Creatures Hiding All Around Us by Hélène Rajcak and Damien Laverdunt

The Marvellous Adventure of Being Human, Your Amazing Body and How to Live in it by Dr Max Pemberton, illustrated by Chris Madden

The History of Prehistory, An Adventure Through 4 Billion Years of Life on Earth by Mick Manning and Brita Granström

Cookery and food

Foods of the World by Libby Walden, illustrated by Jocelyn Kao

The Usborne Book of Growing Food by Abigail Wheatley, Ann Betts and John Russell

Living on the Veg: A Kids' Guide to Life Without Meat by Joe Archer and Caroline Craig

The World in My Kitchen by Sally Brown and Kate Morris

Tilly's Kitchen Takeover by Matilda Ramsay

Edible Science by National Geographic Kids

Ages 9–11

General

The Stick Book / The Wild Weather Book / The Beach Book / The Wild City Book by Fiona Danks and Jo Schofield

Kids Fight Plastic by Martin Dorey, illustrated by Tim Wesson

Recordomania by Sarah Tavernier, Alexandre Verhille and
    Emanuelle Figueras
The School of Art by Teal Triggs and Daniel Frost / *The School
    of Music* by Meurig and Rachel Bowen
H.O.U.S.E. by Aleksandra and Daniel Mizieliński
Absolutely Everything! by Christopher Lloyd
Outside: Discovering Animals / Exploring Nature by Maria Ana
    Peixe Dias, Inês Teixeira Do Rosário and Bernardo P.
    Carvalho
The Way Things Work Now by David Macaulay
Stories for South Asian Supergirls by Raj Kaur Khaira
Stories for Boys Who Dare to Be Different by Ben Brookes,
    illustrated by Quinton Winter

Cookery and food

The Kew Gardens Children's Cookbook by Joe Archer and
    Caroline Craig
The Forest Feast for Kids by Erin Gleeson
Cooks and Kids by Andrew Isaac and Gregg Wallace
Let's Bake by Cathryn Dresser
Science Experiments You Can Eat by Vicki Cobb, illustrated
    by Tad Carpenter
The Kitchen Science Cookbook by Dr Michelle Dickinson
Kitchen Science Lab for Kids: Edible Edition by Liz Lee
    Heinecke

SOUND AND PICTURES: ENJOYING THE VARIETIES OF READING
Ages 3–5

Picture books

Anna Hibiscus' Song / *Splash! Anna Hibiscus* / *Double Trouble for Anna Hibiscus* by Atinuke, illustrated by Lauren Tobia

Ruby's Worry / *Ravi's Roar* by Tom Percival

A Bit Lost / *Oh No, George* / *Shh! We Have a Plan* / *Goodnight Everyone* / *Don't Worry, Little Crab* by Chris Haughton

Cyril, the Lonely Cloud by Tim Hopgood

A Brave Bear by Sean Taylor, illustrated by Emily Hughes

Blue Penguin by Petr Horáček

Jabari Jumps by Gaia Cornwall

Hello, Friend! by Rebecca Cobb

On Sudden Hill by Linda Sarah, illustrated by Benji Davies

Graphic texts, comics and graphic novels

Hug / *Yes* by Jez Alborough

Don't Let the Pigeon Drive the Bus / *Don't Let the Pigeon Stay up Late* / *The Pigeon Needs a Bath* / *The Pigeon Wants a Puppy* / *The Pigeon Finds a Hot Dog* / *The Duckling Gets a Cookie?!* by Mo Willems

Audiobooks

Four Tales from Percy's Park by Nick Butterworth, read by Richard Briers

The Gruffalo and Other Stories by Julia Donaldson, read by
Imelda Staunton, Steven Pacey, Jim Carter and Julia
Donaldson

The Tiger Who Came to Tea and Other Stories by Judith Kerr,
read by Geraldine McEwan, Phyllida Law and Susan
Sheridan

Alfie Gets in First and Other Stories by Shirley Hughes, read
by Roger Allam and Roy McMillan

The Very Hungry Caterpillar and Other Stories by Eric Carle,
read by Roger McGough and Juliet Stevenson

The Elmer Treasury by David McKee, read by Stephen
Thorne

Dogger by Shirley Hughes, read by Olivia Coleman

Frog and Toad Audio Collection by Arnold Lobel, read by
Arnold Lobel

Up and Down by Oliver Jeffers, read by Richard E. Grant

Storytime, First Tales for Sharing retold by Stella Blackstone,
read by Jim Broadbent

Ages 5-7

Picture books

The Secret Sky Garden by Linda Sarah, illustrated by Fiona
Lumbers

How to Find Gold / How to Be on the Moon by Viviane Schwarz

If All the World Were... by Joseph Coelho, illustrated by
Allison Colpoys

Croc and Bird by Alexis Deacon

How to Be a Lion by Ed Vere

The Robot and the Bluebird by David Lucas

The Storm Whale by Benji Davies

The Story Machine by Tom McLaughlin

I Want My Hat Back / This is Not My Hat / We Found a Hat by Jon Klassen

The Tree by Neal Layton

Graphic texts, comics and graphic novels

There are Cats in this Book / There are No Cats in this Book / Is There a Dog in this Book? by Viviane Schwarz

A Place to Call Home by Alexis Deacon and Viviane Schwarz

Banana! by Ed Vere

The New Neighbours by Sarah McIntyre

Traction Man is Here / Traction Man Meets Turbodog / Traction Man and the Beach Odyssey by Mini Grey

Today I Will Fly by Mo Willems

Audiobooks

Hairy Maclary Story Collection by Lynley Dodd, read by David Tennant

The Paddington Treasury for the Very Young by Michael Bond, read by Jim Broadbent

Happy Families: The Audio Collection by Allan Ahlberg, read by Alexander Armstrong

The Big Mog Collection by Judith Kerr, read by Geraldine McEwan and Andrew Sachs

Funnybones by Janet and Allan Ahlberg, read by Stephen Mangan

The Worst Witch by Jill Murphy, read by Gemma Arterton

The Owl Who Was Afraid of the Dark by Jill Tomlinson, read by Bill Oddie

Oi Frog! / Oi Dog! / Oi Cat! / Oi Puppies! by Kes Gray and Jim Field, read by David Mitchell

The Princess and the White Bear King by Tanya Robyn Batt, read by Miranda Richardson

Claude in the City by Alex T. Smith, read by Simon Callow

Ages 7-9
Picture books

Into the Forest by Anthony Browne

Grandad's Island by Benji Davies

The King Who Banned the Dark by Emily Haworth-Booth

Wild by Emily Hughes

Ocean Meets Sky by The Fan Brothers

Black Dog by Levi Pinfold

The Tin Forest by Helen Ward, illustrated by Wayne Anderson

Leaf by Sandra Dieckmann

Here I Am by Patti Kim, illustrated by Sonia Sanchez

The Promise by Nicola Davies, illustrated by Laura Carlin

Graphic texts, comics and graphic novels

Mouse, Bird, Snake, Wolf by David Almond, illustrated by
    Dave McKean

The Getaway by Ed Vere

The Snowman / Ug by Raymond Briggs

Vern and Lettuce by Sarah McIntyre

Azzi In Between by Sarah Garland

*Arthur and the Golden Rope / Marcy and the Riddle of the Sphinx
    / Kai and the Monkey King* by Joe Todd-Stanton

*Hilda and the Troll / Hilda and the Midnight Giant / Hilda and
    the Bird Parade / Hilda and the Black Hound / Hilda and the
    Stone Forest / Hilda and the Mountain King* by Luke Pearson

Evil Emperor Penguin (The Phoenix Presents) by Laura Ellen
    Anderson

Claire, Justice Ninja (The Phoenix Presents) by Joe Brady,
    illustrated by Kate Ashwin

Moomin: The Complete Tove Jansson Comic Strip by Tove
    Jansson

Audiobooks

How to Train Your Dragon by Cressida Cowell, read by David
    Tennant

The Lost Words by Robert Macfarlane and Jackie Morris,
    read by Guy Garvey, Cerys Matthews, Benjamin
    Zephaniah and Edith Bowman

Clarice Bean, Utterly Me by Lauren Child, read by Claire
    Skinner
Planet Omar, Accidental Trouble Magnet by Zanib Mian, read
    by Waleed Akhtar
Boy Giant, Son of Gulliver by Michael Morpurgo, read by
    Akbar Kurtha
You've Been Were-Wolfed by Tom McLaughlin, read by
    Charlie Sanderson
Varjak Paw by S. F. Said, read by Andrew Sachs
Goth Girl series by Chris Riddell, read by Lucy Brown and
    Helen Keeley
The Bolds by Julian Clary, read by Julian Clary
The Boy Who Climbed into the Moon by David Almond, read by
    Malcolm Hamilton

Ages 9–11
Picture books
Red in the City by Marie Voigt
Varmints by Helen Ward, illustrated by Marc Craste
The Journey by Francesca Sanna
Rose Blanche by Roberto Innocenti
The Viewer by Gary Crew, illustrated by Shaun Tan
Way Home by Libby Hathorn, illustrated by Gregory Rogers
The Dam by David Almond, illustrated by Levi Pinfold
Fox by Margaret Wild, illustrated by Ron Brooks

Town is by the Sea by Joanne Schwarz, illustrated by Sydney Smith

King of the Sky by Nicola Davies, illustrated by Laura Carlin

Graphic texts, comics and graphic novels

Ethel and Ernest / When the Wind Blows by Raymond Briggs

Jim's Lion by Russell Hoban, illustrated by Alexis Deacon

El Deafo by Cece Bell

Travels of an Extraordinary Hamster by Astrid Desbordes and Pauline Martin

Roller Girl / All's Faire in Middle School by Victoria Jamieson

Nightlights / Hicotea by Lorena Alvarez

Amulet (9 Volume series) by Kazu Kabuishi

Space Dumplins by Craig Thompson

Stormbreaker: The Graphic Novel by Anthony Horowitz, Antony Johnston, illustrated by Kanako and Yuzuru

Tom's Midnight Garden by Philippa Pearce and Edith

Audiobooks

Harry Potter series by J. K. Rowling, read by Stephen Fry

Cosmic by Frank Cottrell-Boyce, read by Daniel Ryan

The Middler by Kirsty Applebaum, read by Adjoa Andoh

Coraline by Neil Gaiman, read by Dawn French

Murder Most Unladylike by Robin Stevens, read by Gemma Chan

Goodnight Mr Tom by Michelle Magorian, read by Patrick Malahide

Wolf Brother by Michelle Paver, read by Sir Ian McKellen

Street Child by Berlie Doherty, read by Antonia Beamish

The Boy Who Swam with Piranhas by David Almond, read by Malcolm Hamilton

The Girl of Ink and Stars by Kiran Millwood Hargrave, read by Victoria Fox

Acknowledgements

Thanks to Liz Woabank, Abbie Day, Robert Davies, Neil Stevens, Sandra Friesen, Julia Eccleshare and John Lee, as well as Fiona Evans at the National Literacy Trust, the Centre for Literacy in Primary Education, and all the expert contributors and interviewees.